THOMAS HODGSKIN

ÉLIE HALÉVY

THOMAS HODGSKIN

Edited in Translation
With an Introduction by
A. J. TAYLOR

LONDON
ERNEST BENN LIMITED

First Published 1956 by Ernest Benn Limited
Bouverie House · Fleet Street · London · E C 4

Printed in Great Britain

Contents

Author's Foreword

"Hodgskin's illustrious disciple, Karl Marx" —the words are those of the Webbs in their *History of Trade Unionism.* But Karl Marx has had so many masters and of such differing kinds that one would like to know in what ways and to what extent he was influenced by Thomas Hodgskin. My study will perhaps help to throw light on these questions and at the same time make known a forgotten but original thinker of interest in his own right. I shall confine myself, in telling the history of Hodgskin's social and economic ideas, to presenting, in as logical an order as possible, a series of relevant quotations taken from unpublished letters, out-of-print pamphlets and anonymous articles scattered among the periodicals of the mid-nineteenth century. Miss Mary D. Hodgskin has thrown light on several obscure points in the life of her father; M. Pierre Muret, agrégé de l'Université, has very kindly made some further investigations at the British Museum for me.

Translator's Introduction

Elie Halévy is one of that small company of historians who have so made the study of a corner of another nation's history their own that the native historian gladly recognises their authority and pre-eminence. For Halévy, a Frenchman, the other nation was England and the period the nineteenth century: beyond this, particularisation becomes difficult. The whole field of English nineteenth-century history was his parish. Whether in the world of ideas, of institutions or events, in the sphere of politics, of economics or religion he brought a new light to bear on English history; and the pre-eminent place of his works in the bibliographies of later historians is testimony to the position of authority which they came to attain. Halévy's reputation is based largely on two works—*La Formation du Radicalisme Philosophique en Angleterre* and the *Histoire du Peuple Anglais aux dix-neuvième siècle*. Between these two lengthy and monumental works came his only other book on a specifically English theme, the much smaller, though no less thorough, *Thomas Hodgskin*.

This small volume is the study of "a forgotten thinker", an Englishman who, less than half a century after his death, had so slipped into oblivion that his compatriots did not find him worthy of a place in the *Dictionary of National Biography*. Why, then, did Halévy set himself the task of rescuing Hodgskin from this obscurity, and what place does this volume occupy in his life-work? The questions demand investigation if only in order that the study of Hodgskin may be appreciated for what it really is and that it may take its proper place alongside Halévy's other better-known works.

Born in 1870 and entering the École Normale in Paris in 1890, Halévy revealed himself from the outset as a man "with an austere mind, with a philosophic passion which had always a moral cast and a moral purpose . . . always connected with a profound interest in the inner springs and motives of actual contemporary life".[1] These qualities were to express themselves throughout his life and work; they are to be found as clearly in an essay like *Thomas Hodgskin* as in the wider areas of his writing and teaching. By the time he was twenty-one Halévy was engaged on a parallel study of Pascal and Spinoza, evidence both of the nature of his philosophical interests and the beginnings of that preoccupation with the relationship and transmission of ideas which was to play so large a part in his subsequent writings on philosophical and allied subjects, and which was to be the underlying theme of his book on Hodgskin. In 1896 there appeared Halévy's first book, *La Théorie Platonicienne des Sciences*; and by 1898 he was teaching at the École des Sciences Politiques and preparing the theses for his doctorate. The subjects are highly significant.

[1] E. Barker, "Élie Halévy", *English Historical Review*, liii (1938), p. 79.

His Latin thesis was concerned with the psychological theory of the association of ideas, a subject which he had been led to study in the writings of David Hume: his second thesis dealt with Bentham's life and thought and this was in fact to be the first volume of his great work on Philosophical Radicalism. The two theses were, of course, not unconnected. Bentham acknowledged his debt to Hume who may be said to have been his forerunner in the development of both a theory of association and a theory of utility. The theses also emphasise Halévy's growing interest in the relationship of ideas; he traced the influence of French eighteenth-century thought on the development of English utilitarian philosophy and the further close links between utilitarianism and classical economic theory in England.

It was to Taine, the French historian, that Halévy owed his entry into English intellectual society. Taine provided him with an introduction to Leslie Stephen, who was himself engaged on a work on the English Utilitarians. The use which Halévy made of this introduction may be compared with that which Thomas Hodgskin had made of his to J.-B. Say in Paris. Hodgskin, Halévy tells us, failed to take advantage of his introduction to Say to extend his circle of acquaintances: Halévy, on the other hand, quickly established contact with the world of philosophers and historians in England, making not merely acquaintances but friends of a great number of distinguished men and women. Among these were Henry Sidgwick and J. T. E. MacTaggart, Bertrand Russell, Lowes Dickinson, Sidney Ball,

Graham Wallas and the Webbs, H. A. L. Fisher, G. M. Trevelyan and J. L. Hammond. The assessment of their influence on Halévy would be a subject of fruitful investigation, and one in which, by its nature, no one would have been more interested than Halévy himself. No consideration of it is possible here, but it is at least important to note that Halévy was one of a group of scholars who, round about 1900, were examining the foundations of political and economic thought on which nineteenth-century English society had largely been built. An old order was passing away; new theories of economic and social policy were demanding examination and trial; and as men formulated new bases for political and economic action, they re-examined the foundations on which the existing society had been established. The scholars who were thus drawn to the study of philosophical radicalism in its different forms make an imposing list, including as they do, Edwin Cannan, John Rae, Graham Wallas, Leslie Stephen, Élie Halévy himself, A. V. Dicey, and Frank Podmore,[1] each of whom between 1893 and 1906 made a substantial contribution to the history of early nineteenth-century thought and thinkers.

The new approaches being made to economic and

[1] Cannan, *A History of the theories of production and distribution in English political economy from 1776 to 1848* (1893); Rae, *Life of Adam Smith* (1895); Wallas, *The Life of Francis Place 1771–1854* (1898); Stephen, *The English Utilitarians* (1900); Halévy, *La Formation du Radicalisme Philosophique en Angleterre* (1900–04); *Thomas Hodgskin, 1787–1869* (1903); Dicey, *Lectures on the Relation between Law and Public Opinion in England during the Nineteenth Century* (1905); Podmore, *Life of Robert Owen* (1906).

social problems were the response of thinkers to a changing balance of forces in contemporary society. The extension of the franchise to all male adults in 1884—with its creation of the highly significant miners' vote—and the emergence of the mass industrial trade union in the early 1890s had at last begun to shake the foundations of middle-class England. The England of the years between the first and second Reform Acts had been essentially the England of the classical economists and the Benthamite radicals, of *laissez-faire* and utilitarianism. In no previous period of England's development had the teachings of economists and social philosophers been so assiduously applied by legislators and administrators. But by the eighteen-sixties the inner contradictions of Philosophical Radicalism had begun to show themselves. In fostering the desire for a widening franchise utilitarianism not only began to undermine the middle-class control of government but also opened up the way for the advance of the forces of paternalism and collectivism. The Reform Act of 1867, therefore, meant the beginning of the end of middle-class dominance. On its heels came equally significant, though not necessarily related, developments—the Trade Union legislation of 1871 and 1875, J. S. Mill's refutation of the Wages Fund theory in 1869 and the publication by W. S. Jevons of the *Theory of Political Economy* in 1871, with its deposition of the labour—or cost of production—theory of value in favour of that based on the concept of marginal utility. But while both in the world of economic and social theory and in that of affairs, the established order continued to make concessions during the eighteen-seventies and eighties, these concessions were essentially peripheral and in no sense fundamentally altered either the classical orthodox foundations of political economy or the middle-class character of English government. Even Marshall's *Principles*, for all its breadth and originality, was, on his own statement, "an attempt to present a modern version of old doctrines"[1] and had its firm roots in classical orthodoxy; nor by the late eighteen-eighties had the challenge of the inflammatory ideas of the *Communist Manifesto* and the first two volumes of *Capital* made a visible impression on the political and economic dominance of the English middle class.

The eighteen-nineties, however, saw a change. For two decades theory and practice had been drifting apart. Now they were drawn together again almost as surely as they had been in the heyday of Philosophical Radicalism. The Fabians, wedding the socialist economics of Marx and his predecessors to the "new economics" of Jevons and Marshall, and carrying their ideas into the councils of the political parties, were the agents of this reconciliation. Thus, although the full harvest of Fabian "permeation" was not reaped until after 1945, striking parallels are to be observed between the era of emergent Fabianism at the end of the nineteenth century and the earlier age of Benthamism; and it is not surprising that, in the new period of change, reflective students of current affairs should have cast their minds back to the earlier age of reform and of new beginnings. As they did so some

[1] T. H. Marshall, *Principles of Economics*, 8th edn. (1920), p. v.

of them also paused to examine the abortive attempts of the early English socialists to establish, before 1850, that proletarian society whose creation now engaged the energies of the Fabian and other socialist groups. Among these historians were Frank Podmore, writing the definitive life of Robert Owen, and Élie Halévy, studying the thought of Thomas Hodgskin.

Thomas Hodgskin was written while the final volume of *La Formation du Radicalisme Philosophique* was making its way through the press. By the end of 1904 the three volumes of the major work and its smaller companion were in print and Halévy, at the age of thirty-four, had already made a contribution to the history of English thought sufficient to place him in the first rank of historians. But he knew that his work was only beginning, and the pattern of his life, now becoming firmly established, bears witness to the fact. Each autumn he began his course of lectures at the École des Sciences Politiques, delivering in alternate years lectures on either Socialism or England. Every year new material gave added vitality to the courses. By Easter the teaching session was at an end and Halévy with his wife came to England. In London he and Madame Halévy spent their days working in the great libraries—in the Reading and Newspaper Rooms of the British Museum, in the Public Record Office, and among the Bentham Manuscripts at University College—and conversing with their many English friends. The demands of examinations brought them back to Paris in July and then the annual cycle began again.

With his writings on radical thought behind him, Halévy was able to look out on wider, unexplored areas. Already in his excursions into the history of nineteenth-century England, he had observed how England had come through a period of fundamental economic and social change without any serious disturbance of her internal peace. He had found no explanation for this in Philosophical Radicalism which, far from encouraging stability, seemed to him to contain the seeds of discord; and therefore he sought for a solution to his problem in other directions. He came to feel that he had discovered it in the growing power of nonconformity and particularly of Wesleyanism in early nineteenth-century England, and it was accordingly to the field of religious thought that he next turned his attention.

But the field was not untended: others were working there, and Halévy concluded that he could make a more useful impact elsewhere. Unhappily the work of these earlier arrivals proved unfruitful, and of the large-scale contribution which Halévy himself would doubtless have made there remains only the earnest of two articles published in the *Revue de Paris* of 1906. This loss, however, was not without compensation. From Wesleyanism Halévy moved to that wider study of English history on which his general reputation in this country is so largely based. He turned to his grand design of examining the history of the English people in the nineteenth century with the particular intention of relating the ideas, whose origin and development he had described and analysed, to institutions and events. The philosopher became historian, but he "only became a historian because he was a philosopher. . . . He always remained a philosopher."[1]

Henceforward, until his death in 1937, the *History* was to occupy almost all his writing-time; but not all his interest. Alongside his nineteenth-century research there stood, on the one hand, his fundamental interest in philosophical questions, finding expression in the editorship of the *Revue de métaphysique et de morale*, and, with it, his allied interest in socialism; and, on the other, his interest in current affairs, receiving stimulus from the invitation to give the Rhodes Lectures of 1930 at Oxford. Indeed his investigations in history and in current affairs marched ever closer together. The final two volumes of the *History* covered the years from 1895 to 1915, a period coincident with the first half of his own teaching career; and the material for this study had been gathered as the events themselves unfolded. It was from the vantage point of these years that he had earlier written the history of the first half of the nineteenth century, surveying one age of change from the standpoint of another. Now, after 1923, he turned his attention to that period of breaking and making through which he, himself, had lived, to view it as the *Epilogue* to a century which had been for him "the culmination, or to speak less dogmatically, one of the culminations of British culture".[2] To the last his fundamental interest lay in the history of ideas rather than of events. He had described the growth of ideas in the first half of the nineteenth century and their disintegration as a new

[1] E. Barker, *op. cit.*, p. 80.

[2] *Histoire du Peuple Anglais; Epilogue* (1926), p. ii.

century began. When he began to write the last, unfinished volume of the *History* covering the years from 1841 to 1852, he felt that he was "realising the essential of his design. He would at least have followed through the growth of an age whose end was explained by his Epilogue."[1]

* * * * *

If Halévy's creative life is divided into two periods around his two great works, the first or "philosophical" one is that to which the study of *Thomas Hodgskin* clearly belongs. The essay was at once an appendix to his work on the Philosophical Radicals and a by-product of the intensive study of socialist origins which he was undertaking at this time for the course on socialism at the École des Sciences Politiques. It was a study of a man who was both within and without the utilitarian fold, a heretic who claimed to be professing the faith more loyally than the priests themselves, who condemned Bentham and Ricardo, not for errors in their principles but for inconsistencies in their pursuit of them, and yet who, at the same time, without knowing or willing it, was preparing the ground for Marxian socialism. This essay, therefore, provided a common focal point for three of Halévy's greatest intellectual interests—utilitarianism, socialism and the relationship of ideas.

Thomas Hodgskin is the study of the development of a man's ideas: it is not the history of his life and times. Those who turn to this volume for biography

[1] *Vide* P. Vaucher, "Élie Halévy," *Revue Historique*, clxxx (1937), p. 425.

or for history in the more general sense will be disappointed: only such essential events in Hodgskin's life as are necessary to the understanding of his thought are to be found here. This was not altogether a matter of choice for Halévy. Much of the detail of Hodgskin's life story remains obscure, not because Halévy wished it so, but because the evidence for a fuller reconstruction is lacking. This subordination of contemporary life and of action to thought could, in the study of many thinkers, prove disastrous. Locke, for example, cannot be made fully comprehensible except against the setting of the English Revolution of the seventeenth century; and a knowledge of the personal as well as the public background of Rousseau's life is vital to a complete appreciation of the development of his political philosophy. Of Hodgskin, however, this is far less true. Born in the decade of the French Revolution and of the first steam-powered mill, he came to manhood in the shadow of these two portentous events. But it was essentially the shadow rather than the substance with which he was familiar. His democracy—for in spite of his fundamental anarchism, he professed himself a democrat—derived from the English Revolution of the seventeenth century rather than from the French of the eighteenth; and the basis for his excursions in economic thought, like those of his master, Adam Smith, was a world not yet dominated by the steam-engine and the factory system. He made a tour of philosophical investigation through France, Italy, Switzerland and Germany, but seems to have made only one journey of any length in his own country—along the North

Road from London to Edinburgh, which, at all points, lay well to the east of the great new industrial regions of early nineteenth-century England. Like Bentham and Ricardo he knew both French and Industrial Revolutions at second-hand and from a distance, and his thought and writing reflect the fact.[1]

If the fundamental changes of his age laid only light hands upon Hodgskin, he was more closely touched by immediate events, some of which impinged closely on his personal life: but even in these instances his thought was comparatively little affected by his experiences. Fighting at Copenhagen and victimised for his courageous attack on the excesses of naval discipline, actively engaged in the struggle for the repeal of the Combination Acts and of the Corn Laws and instructing his wife in the use of a warning pistol during the tumultuous days of 1831 and 1832, sharing for a time in the advocacy of Chartism and opposing Macaulay's Education Bill, his was far from being the life of a recluse. In an age of radical agitation his sympathies were readily aroused and his pen enlisted on behalf of the underprivileged. But if his writings were sometimes occasioned by events, his thought was little influenced by them. *Labour defended against the claims of Capital*, written as it was to support the movement for the repeal of the Combination Acts, is essentially a work

[1] This is not to say that Hodgskin was unaware of the extent or the economic significance of the changes that were taking place in nineteenth century England (see *Popular Political Economy*, *passim*); but his lack of direct contact with the industrial areas gave to his treatment of their problems a theoretical rather than a practical bent.

of theory based on Hodgskin's reaction to the thoughts of others—a reaction determined largely by Hodgskin's peculiar temperament; and such is the case with all his work. Hodgskin admitted almost as much at one stage in a letter which Halévy has quoted (page 34). It is only just, however, to state that on a later occasion Hodgskin criticised Ricardo and his followers for their failure to use history to test their theories and thereby implied that his own approach was historical. In a measure this is true: but Hodgskin's methodology in history was essentially deductive, the approach of a philosopher with an *a priori* thesis to be illustrated rather than that of a scientific historian.

Hodgskin remained to the last, unlike Place or Owen, a man of the study rather than of the market-place. Though he had a considerable if ephemeral influence over sections of the working-class—Place compared him with Owen in this respect—he had no aspirations to leadership among men, and, when time dimmed the immediate popularity of his ideas and subsequently bequeathed them to others for development, he made no complaint. Significantly his only grievance against posterity was that it appeared to be giving to Lord Brougham the credit for the establishment of the Mechanics' Institute which Hodgskin felt rightly belonged to himself.

In one direction, however, the interaction between events and temperament served to clarify and strengthen, if not to occasion, Hodgskin's ideas. His encounters with authority in its various shapes and forms were almost uniformly unhappy. How far his childhood relations with his father coloured his later thinking can only be guessed; but it is clear that his experiences of naval discipline and its results helped to breed or confirm in him a mistrust of man-made authority and laws. The subsequent years of unemployment, the disappointments surrounding the establishment of the Mechanics' Institute and, when he was still barely forty, the rejection of his application for a chair at the newly-founded London University[1] probably served to intensify his prejudice against the powers that be. His own reserve and self-effacement—or timidity, if one will —was no doubt a contributory factor to these failures and disappointments; but, whatever their cause, it seems probable that they developed in Hodgskin that latent bitterness towards established authority, which lay at the root of his anarchism. In following out the logic of his fundamentally anarchic approach he was led to take up positions where he could make little practical contribution to the problems of a changing society and to leave to others—of whom Marx was one—the elaboration of incidental reflections whose pragmatic importance has proved considerable. But without the fundamental anarchic bias with which Hodgskin approached the thought of the Philosophical Radicals, it is probable that he would have become, like so many of his contemporaries, a mere retailer of half-truths derived at second hand from the teaching of Bentham and Ricardo.

Hodgskin's anarchism, therefore, fed on his personal disappointments; but, this apart, the development of his ideas owed surprisingly little to his

[1] *Vide* the note on *The Word BELIEF defined and explained* at the end of the bibliography of this volume (pp. 190–2).

peculiar personal experiences, and, though one would wish that more evidence had survived of the life of this courageous and highly conscientious radical, such evidence would probably add little to our understanding of him as a thinker. Halévy's study, therefore, achieves its purpose. He has largely allowed Hodgskin to speak for himself, selecting salient passages from his published books, articles and reviews, and supplementing these with lengthy quotations from his correspondence. In the concluding chapter, however, Halévy moves on to what was essentially the mainspring of his study—a consideration of the relationship of Hodgskin to two great thinkers of the next generation, Spencer and Marx. Here he is on controversial ground; how controversial is indicated by the reaction of Spencer to the suggestion that his ideas proceeded from those of Hodgskin. The octogenarian philosopher, in letters to Mary Hodgskin, rejected this view; but Halévy's thesis in this instance appears to rest on a basis that is at least circumstantially convincing. The case of Marx is different, for Marx was no despiser of other men's opinions and freely buttressed his arguments with quotations from authorities great and small. Hence the problem is not to find precursors to Marx, but to distinguish the significant from the insignificant. Halévy, in penetrating beneath the immediate and admitted debt of Marx to Hodgskin in economic questions to his debt at more fundamental philosophical levels, was opening up questions which have engaged the attention of many thinkers in the present century.

It would be impossible—as well as impertinent—

to attempt to review here the subsequent development of the many-sided discussion of Marxist origins. It is quite clear, however, that, setting aside the question of the degree of direct indebtedness of Marx to Hodgskin and his socialist contemporaries, Hodgskin anticipated Marx, not only in propounding a theory of surplus-value, but also in implying a class interpretation of history. Consider the following passage from *Labour defended against the claims of Capital*.

> In all errors which are generally adopted there is a tolerable substratum of truth. In the present case the substratum of truth is this: There was a time in society when CAPITAL and CAPITALISTS were of most essential service to it. On the establishment of towns in Europe, and on the introduction of manufactures into them, they became the refuge of all the oppressed and enslaved peasantry who could escape from their feudal tyrants. The capitalists and manufacturers who inhabited them were also skilled labourers, and really gave employment and protection to the peasantry. They taught them useful arts, and hence became invested with the character of benefactors, both to the poor and the state. They were infinitely better than the feudal barons with whom they were compared; and the character they then acquired they now retain. The veneration men have for CAPITAL and CAPITALISTS is founded on a sort of superstitious and transmitted notion of their utility in former times. But they have long since reduced the ancient tyrant of the soil to comparative insignificance, while they have inherited his power over all the labouring classes. It is, therefore, now time that the reproaches so long cast on the feudal aristocracy should be heaped on capital and capitalists; or on that still more oppressive aristocracy which is founded on wealth, and which is nourished by profit.[1]

[1] *Labour defended*, p. 19 (footnote).

Marx was only seven when this was written. If, when twenty years later he began to apply the Hegelian dialectic to the development of economic society Marx found this similar approach to history in an independent, non-Hegelian source, its effect must have been at least to strengthen, if not to suggest, the course of his own thinking. This is not to say that Hodgskin merits the anachronistic appellation of Marxist, still less that of revolutionary socialist. His socialism foreshadows the gradualness of the Fabians rather than the open class conflict of *The Communist Manifesto* (cf. *The Natural and Artificial Rights of Property contrasted*, p. 101, cited by Halévy, p. 125).

Nor was this the only point at which Hodgskin opened up lines of economic thought undeveloped by Marx. Both in his division of the functions of the entrepreneur into those of capitalist and manager and in his closely-reasoned criticism, fifty years before Marshall, of Ricardo's conception of rent, he anticipated important developments in later economic theory. Yet these were for him false trails, hares started never to be pursued: Hodgskin's lineal successor was not Marx, still less Marshall, but the anarchist Herbert Spencer.

Hodgskin remains, nevertheless, of outstanding interest as an individual whose thought and writings mirror the dichotomy existing in the philosophical system of the utilitarians, thereby revealing the diverging pathways which led from Bentham and Ricardo to the extremes of collectivism on the one hand and of individualism on the other. The precise role played by Hodgskin in this process of transmission and diversification must remain a matter of controversy: but, if only in raising the problem, Halévy achieved an end far broader than the biographical title of his essay might suggest.

* * * * *

In making this translation I have taken every care to restore Hodgskin's own words where they are the subject of quotation. In all except one or two minor instances this has proved possible either by direct reference to printed word and manuscript or, in the case of those letters which remained in the possession of the Hodgskin family, by the use of Halévy's well-preserved transcripts. Occasionally where Halévy has paraphrased I have taken the liberty of restoring Hodgskin's original phrasing—not that in any of these instances the effect of the paraphrase was to falsify or obscure the original. In the case of the letters, I have retained all those grammatical errors, misspellings and inconsistent usages of capitals that may creep in to writing which the author intends should go no further than the immediate recipient; but for the reader's convenience I have modified the erratic and spasmodic punctuation. (Those who would wish to read Hodgskin's prose at its best should turn to his *Labour defended against the claims of Capitalism*, most recently reprinted with an introduction by G. D. H. Cole in 1923.) A small number of misprints and faulty references in the original have been corrected and I have also taken the opportunity of adding to the bibliography details of certain published works of and about Hodgskin which have come to light or been written since 1903.

My colleagues, Professor A. B. C. Cobban and Dr. C. Smith, by reading through and commenting on parts of my manuscript during its preparation, have given me valuable assistance which I gladly acknowledge. Needless to say, however, all responsibility for this volume is mine. To Madame Florence Halévy I owe an especial debt, not only for placing her husband's notes at my disposal—including his correspondence with Hodgskin's daughter, Miss Mary Hodgskin—but for answering many questions about his life and work.

A. J. TAYLOR

CHAPTER ONE

1787 – 1823

Childhood – Years at Sea – *Essay on Naval Discipline* (1813) – Continental Journey: *Travels in the North of Germany* (1820) – Years in Edinburgh and Correspondence with Francis Place (1819–22)

Thomas Hodgskin was born on 12 December 1787 at Chatham where his father was storekeeper in the naval dockyard. Between a selfish, vain and spendthrift father, who on a salary of £700 ended up by reducing his family to poverty, and a mother, who for thirty years struggled patiently but vainly to conceal the thriftlessness and misconduct of the head of the family, Thomas with his brothers and sisters had a childhood without joys and pleasures.[1] Moreover, when he was barely twelve, his father cut short his education and, deciding to shake off responsibility for him, took advantage of the influence which he enjoyed through his Admiralty post to send the boy to sea as a cadet on a warship. For twelve years Thomas Hodgskin was a sailor, cruising in the Mediterranean along the coasts of Africa, where he was able to observe primi-

[1] Hodgskin to Place, Paris, undated, but July 1816. [Unless otherwise indicated, all letters quoted in this chapter were (1903) in the possession of the Hodgskin family and were made available by Miss Mary Hodgskin.—*Translator*.]

tive forms of exchange among the wild tribes of the area,[1] and in the Northern Seas, where in 1801[2] he distinguished himself during the Copenhagen expedition. He read all he could; but his books were chosen, he tells us, haphazardly, as is the way with sailors.[3]

> Reflection should follow the acquisition of knowledge but I began to reflect in the midnight watch, on the solitary deck, on the wide ocean, amidst the wildest or the most peaceable scenes of nature . . . the dead calm of the tropics or the storms of winter, before I had acquired a sufficient stock of material.[4]

He had no intellectual sympathy for the comrades among whom he had been thrown by his father's whim, and no inclination for the profession which had been thrust upon him. The discipline of a sailor's life accorded neither with his temperament nor with the principles which he had already adopted. "I had decided," he tells us, "to make a powerful resistance to oppression every time I was its victim." For a long time, however, he went on obeying reluctantly, either out of cowardice or from force of habit. But one day, at last, he could contain himself no longer. "I complained," he wrote, "of the injury done me, by a commander-in-chief, to himself, in the language that I thought it merited; he had unjustly deprived me of every chance of promotion from my own exertions, and that was robbing me of every hope."[5] By this outburst

[1] *Popular Political Economy*, p. 153.
[2] [The original has 1807, a curious error.]
[3] *Essay on Naval Discipline*, p. xxiv.
[4] Hodgskin to Place, Paris, 21 March 1816.
[5] *Nav. Disc.*, p. xiii.

Hodgskin worsened his position. He was put on the retired list at half-pay. Though he was barely twenty-five, circumstances had already made him "a discontented and disappointed man".[1]

> The absurdity of its [the navy's] laws and customs has deeply injured myself. My opinion of these is so irretrievably bad, that, in common with many others, I feel no shame at having fallen under their lash—and but that they have deprived me of the good opinion of Society, which is too generally built upon success; but that they have partially deprived me of the esteem of my *friends*; and, but that they have completely excluded me from that road to fame and fortune, the navy, in which my whole life has been past [*sic*], I should not have felt *punishment* an injury. Having received so deep an injury from these laws, it has become a positive duty in me to attempt to alter *them* through the medium of public *opinion*.[2]

He fulfilled this duty when, in 1813, he published *An Essay on Naval Discipline*, in which he set down the results of his experience of a sailor's life. In this work he claims himself to be the disciple of Locke, of Paley and of Malthus;[3] is there not also ground for believing that he had come under the influence of Godwin, even though he never mentions him? Though a Christian, he sets himself up as an opponent of innate ideas,[4] as a utilitarian, and an individualist.

> Patiently submitting to oppression (because it comes from a superior) is a vice: to surmount your fears of that superior, and resist it, is a virtue. I must conclude so, whether I take utility as the prescribed end of my moral

[1] *Ibid.*, p. xiv.
[2] *Ibid.*, pp. x–xi.
[3] *Ibid.*, pp. 18, 99, 166.
[4] *Ibid.*, p. 74.

duties, or whether I go to the precepts of that religion that tells me to do justice and love mercy; the most sacred kind of justice is that which a man owes to himself, and to do that perfectly, will, in the end, be found most compatible with the real interest and good of society—such conduct may not please an avaricious governor, or a jealous superior, but it strictly accords with that utility which is the end of morality; it is virtuous and will ever remain *virtuous*, while virtue continues to be doing right, according to the extent of your knowledge, in hopes of enjoying eternal happiness.[1]

Experience has taught him, he says, that "mankind are everywhere made alike; that the beneficent Creator of all has given to every man similar passions."[2] If, in spite of that, men differ from one another it is because of circumstances beyond their individual control. Why among all the people in the world are the English the happiest and most virtuous? Because they are better governed than the others or, more precisely, because they are less governed. Why are the men who serve in the English navy marked out by defects from the rest of the nation?[3] Because they are subject to a regime exceptional in its tyranny and arbitrariness. The regime should be reformed, the existing barbarous system of recruitment modified, the press-gang abolished, and short-term engagements introduced. But then how will the required number of men be found? By improving rates of pay so that they accord with the wages paid in other parts of the economy. Wages "are good when they permit a labourer to bring up a family, have the necessaries

[1] *Nav. Disc.*, pp. xii–xiii. Cf. pp. xiv, 168. [2] *Ibid.*, p. x.
[3] *Ibid.*, chap. V and VI.

of life and some few of its luxuries".[1] At the same time, if necessary, laws should be passed restraining luxury. How can men talk of a shortage of man-power for the armed forces when the servants of the rich are so numerous?[2] Property exerts an "unjust and injurious influence"; for "it absolutely (though the proportion may be ever so small) takes from the daily labourer to give to the idle gentleman. . . . The legislature should forbid any man, except for agricultural or manufactural purposes, to keep more than two men servants."[3] But, above all, care must be taken not to abuse the penal laws against sailors. The love of glory is a greater force than the fear of death. It has more influence than a million penal laws. The right to punish, in the absolute form it has come to assume in the navy, amounts to a virtual usurpation of the powers of God.[4]

> The vast authority of general opinion will teach us that too much care cannot be taken to prevent the enacting [of] penal statutes, and it will teach us that mankind will universally become much better by being better thought of.[5]

If there must be punishments, continues Hodgskin, let them at least be punishments determined by unvarying regulations and not subject to the capricious discretion of an officer: let the court martials model themselves on the English courts which "do not punish the innocent, neither . . . suffer the guilty to escape".[6] This was hardly the language of a revolutionary: but the indignation which made Hodgskin an author was none the less a fit of anger

[1] *Ibid.*, p. 187. [2] *Ibid.*, p. 102. [3] *Ibid.*, pp. 173, 192.
[4] *Ibid.*, p. 42. [5] *Ibid.*, p. 16. [6] *Ibid.*, p. 134.

against governmental authority, a desire to protest, on a specific issue, against the injustice of regulations and statutes. A short time afterwards he confessed this cheerfully in a personal letter.

All visionaries from Mme. Kruedener to Mr. Owen and Thomas Hodgskin, who are nourished only by their own thoughts and from whom the very diversity of their opinions too rarely brings them into contact with their fellows, are all confident people, and, knowing nothing beyond their own little circle of knowledge, believe every germ either of passion or of thought to be immutable truth. I think you must be aware that my opinions on this subject were the result of *passion*. I was angry at being punished when I thought I was doing the duty of a good man and a good citizen, but then it was my duty I found not to be there, but a patient good slave. This anger made me read books on the subject, and I sought in vain. I sought and still seek in the writings of celebrated authors for any justification of the *right to punish*, and the result of that was a system of opinion which, as far as I have read, may be called on the whole peculiar.[1]

About this time Hodgskin made the acquaintance of the Charing Cross Road tailor, Francis Place—Place, the Westminster political reformer, the friend of Bentham and of James Mill, and the friend also of William Godwin, now old, debt-ridden and despised. The *Essay on Naval Discipline* may have brought Hodgskin to the notice of the London Radicals. Place describes him as he then knew him: "of rather a gloomy disposition, singularly modest and unobtrusive, easily excited, but much more for mirth than anger, he was speculative and entertained as he still continues to do some very curious meta-

[1] Hodgskin to Place, Dresden, end of 1817.

phisical [*sic*] opinions"[1]—doubtless those on which he based his anti-governmental, "anarchist" system, whose origin we have seen. He was sad because he felt himself as one gone astray, without a career and lacking the practical turn of mind required to make one. We find him at one point in Edinburgh filling up his time by sorting out his ideas on philosophy and writing a treatise on *Mind*.[2] What was his philosophy at this time? Letters which he wrote to Francis Place shortly afterwards allow us to infer it. Against Benthamite Utilitarianism which reduced every deed of virtue to a plain and calculated act of individual prudence, he took up the defence of those moral promptings, which, although doubtless not free from the influence of prejudice and error, are an expression of the total experience of mankind and a prerequisite of knowledge and foresight. Against Benthamite atheism he affirmed the existence of God—not the God of the priests and persecutors but the unchanging providence of the laws of nature.

Those perceptions which we call matter are constantly accompanied by signs of the uniformity of this law, by signs of power producing, destroying, preserving and recreating. We infer the existence of the mind of our fellow creatures from signs only: from the signs here enumerated I infer in like manner the existence of a *mind* or *consciousness* constantly connected with matter. Another term for this mind is *God*—for *Matter*, *God* and *Nature* appear to me to be three words nearly synonymous, the first and the last expressing our continued perceptions while the middle one expresses the signs of power bene-

[1] B.M. Add. MSS. 27, 791, f. 268. There are inaccuracies in Place's account.

[2] Place to Mill, 20 July 1815, B.M. Add. MSS. 35, 153, f. 141.

volent and uniform with which they are accompanied. This is my *God*, this also is Berkeley's God, and it is the God of that Scripture writer who said in him we live and move and have our being.[1]

And on this belief in the existence of a providential harmony in nature he finally took his stand to refute Bentham's belief in punishment and to deny the right to punish.

Your friend Mr. Bentham must, I think, remould the commencement of his *Traité* and, adopting the opinions of Berkeley that every individual's sensations are all that is known to himself, come with me to the conclusion that *pain* and *crime* are nearly synonymous and differ only that the latter is applied to the action while the former is its result, and that it is absurd and injust to add another pain, when what every individual feels is the precise and only measure of the crime he has committed.[2]

The manuscript of the treatise, *On Mind*, was sent to Place; but Place did not find a publisher for it. How then was Hodgskin to make a living and occupy his time? With the publication of his pamphlet his service career had been brought to an end: he would remain, till his death, an officer on half-pay, at first as a lieutenant, then as a captain. What, therefore, should he become? A doctor? But for that he must know Latin; and he disliked sciences which involved terminology. A lawyer? For that one must have no feeling for justice. He was aware that he would have to make good his deficiencies of education and he was no longer young enough to do so. At this point he formed a new idea, suggested in all probability by Place who

[1] Hodgskin to Place, Paris, 18 February 1816.

[2] Hodgskin to Place, Rome, 5 February 1817.

had just sent his son to Paris and was himself thinking of spending some time with James Mill on the Continent. He would take advantage of the return of peace to travel through Europe, making a tour of philosophical investigation in the manner of Arthur Young: he would go to study in the European countries the "causes of habits" and the way in which national character is influenced by differences in forms of government.[1] He obtained leave from the Admiralty and set out in July 1815.

He spent many months in Paris, but being, as always, shy and excessively reserved, he failed to make use of an introduction to J.-B. Say to extend his circle of acquaintances. He was too much an Englishman to appreciate the native genius of foreigners; he was put off by French light-heartedness, in which he was tempted to see a perpetual affectation, scandalised by the lack of restraint in speech and manners, and then, when he did get inside a French home, astonished at the simplicity and earnestness of family life. He was, above all, too introspective to make a good observer. Moreover, he received bad news of his family who had been obliged to accept financial assistance from Francis Place. He became sad and weary, but went on formulating his anti-governmental philosophy. He inveighed constantly against the French system of government, against the police, public education and the academies. In the same way he repudiated —so he told Place—the Owenite system in which he

[1] Place to Hodgskin, 22 November 1815. B.M. Add. MSS. 35, 153, f. 184.

also came up against "rules, laws, and what is called order".

> His system . . . supposes masters and servants, somebody to govern as well as somebody to obey and would answer very well in a part of the society while those laws of whose vigour he complains exist to form the minds of some to submit and to protect others in commanding. I suppose that society was generally composed of master-manufacturers and servants and there were no laws to protect the masters but what would be the result of the reason of the whole. The servants, seeing they were as useful to the masters as the masters' capital to them, that each one was mutually necessary to every other to succeed in their joint concern, would insist on an equality of privileges and profit; or the first law of such a society would probably be to abolish that distinction between masters and servants which pervades Mr. Owen's plan and which now exists in consequence of those laws whose effects are so evil.[1]

Already his views on the artificial distribution of wealth had set him apart in his thinking from the Malthusianism of Place and of the other Benthamites: he attacked Gray for confusing two things in his work *On Population*, the quantity of idlers and the quantity of labour.

> Our expenditure has been for the last 30 years enormous. During that period the plan has become general throughout the country to pay people according to their work instead of according to the hours they are employed, the consequence is that a vast deal more work has been done by the same number of people. Of course more goods have been produced. If the country has during that period increased in riches, this has been the immediate cause—and the remote one: the enormous expenditure on idle persons which in some measure compels an increase

[1] Hodgskin to Place, Paris, 20 August 1816.

of labour is confounded with it by Mr. Gray. The state of the people who labour has at last become so wretched as to attract the attention of the Legislator and proves that the oppressions which have compelled them to produce more and thus increase the population have only added to the misery of the mass.[1]

In September Hodgskin left Paris and reached Italy, making his way on foot. As he went he noted the wretchedness of the French peasantry after twenty years of upheaval and war, and the even greater poverty of the Italians. He stayed for some time in Florence, moved on to Rome and then returned north to visit the Po Valley and the Tyrol. But he grew weary of Italy as he had of France. He found too many churches, monuments to southern superstition, too many works of art, about which he declared he understood nothing and which left him "sick at heart",[2] and, on the other hand, too few men who were able to take an interest in truly humane questions and in the problems of politics. Still on foot, he crossed the St. Bernard through the snow and came into Switzerland.

He visited Switzerland, sailed down the Danube by raft as far as Vienna, crossed Bohemia and passed through Saxony and Brandenburg. By this time, on the advice of Place, he had decided to write an account of his travels in the North of Germany; and the long letters which he wrote to Place were nothing more than detailed notes prepared for the later writing of his book. When he reached Hanover in July 1818 he set still further limits to the scope

[1] Hodgskin to Place, Paris, 1816 (undated, probably July).
[2] Hodgskin to Place, Florence, 12 January 1817.

of his work, and, armed with a questionnaire which Bentham had dictated for him to James Mill,[1] undertook an inquiry into the government, religion, trade and agriculture of the country in which he was staying. Then he returned to England along the banks of the Rhine. His journey ended on an unfortunate note: he caught cold, took to his bed on reaching Frankfurt and had scarcely recovered when, having sailed down the Rhine, he arrived at Amsterdam. But he had just taken a step forward in his economic thinking. He had read an article in the *Edinburgh Review* in which MacCulloch commended to the public the newly published *Principles* of Ricardo; and at once he had seen what he could take from Ricardo's theories and on what points he would be at variance with him. He was at one with Ricardo in seeing the quantity of labour as the only source of value; but, even so, he said,

I see no natural cause either why *capital* which is merely the saving of labour and which of itself produces nothing should be considered as affecting real price—if that is always to be considered as accurately measured by the quantity of labour. Capital [should be] considered as either a quantity of those things which men desire or a command over them. Money is one of those things which produces an artificial price instead of a real price. Its profits are merely a portion of the produce of labour which the capitalist, without any other right than what laws give him, takes to himself. What he lends is never anything more than a power to command those necessaries of life, which are necessary to the workman while he produces something which is sufficient to replace what he has con-

[1] The questionnaire is at B.M. Add. MSS. 35, 153, f. 3 ff.

sumed during the time of producing and to leave an overplus for the capitalist.[1]

Some days later he was asking why, to his mind, Friesland was badly farmed; and for this he found two reasons—increased government expenditure and, more important, "the accumulation of capital".

This [i.e. capital] as a means of production can only be those instruments and the necessaries of life which the labourer uses and consumes while he produces. An accumulation of these in the hands of the labourer makes them cheap and makes also what is produced while they are consumed equally cheap. But an accumulation of their representative, money, or even themselves in the hands of persons other than the labourers makes all dear. These persons, the capitalists, without producing, take not only interest from the person who has to labour this land, but the same accumulation allows an interest to be demanded from all other labourers who use this capital. The cultivator must pay, in addition to the real price, also the interest which other labourers pay on all articles he, the cultivator, consumes. . . . I do not mean that a greater quantity of labour will be required to produce, but that every man who produces must give in greater proportion of his productions for those articles which his own labour does not produce. . . . I am a friend to that economy which spares today that tomorrow may not be without food. But I have never been, either from reasoning or from feeling, a friend to that accumulation which, too generally begun in parsimony and injustice, appears to me one of the most powerful means of perpetrating injustice and encouraging, in a few, a prodigious waste to the oppression of the many. I am an enemy of those doctrines of the political economists that praise the accumulation of capital. They lend a sort of reason to that pursuit of wealth which is the present curse of the

[1] Hodgskin to Place, Amsterdam, 25 September 1818.

world. They encourage the rich to make themselves still richer by all sorts of exactions, by persuading them that their accumulations promote the industry and wealth of the whole.[1]

At last, in November 1818, after an absence of three years, Hodgskin reached London. He turned down the requests of Bentham and his followers who wanted him to come to Ford Abbey, the summer residence of the great reformer, to defend and to test in discussion his anarchist philosophy.[2] He set out for Edinburgh where he rejoined a German girl with whom he had fallen in love while in Hanover and who was to be his courageous and intelligent companion for the remaining fifty years of his life.[3] They were married, and at once he began his work. In January 1820 his *Travels in the North of Germany* appeared. Through it one becomes aware of the progress made in his thinking—in preciseness and also in dogmatism—during his six years of travel and reflection.

In the course of his journeys through Germany, Hodgskin had seen the spread of liberal agitation against the Holy Alliance, as a result of French, and perhaps still more, of English inspiration. Travelling on foot he had had no contact with statesmen, diplomats or generals, but had talked with commercial travellers, workers and peasants: he had come to know, not those who made the laws, but those who were subject to them and who paid the

[1] Hodgskin to Place, Amsterdam, 12 October 1818.

[2] Hodgskin to Place, Deptford, 8 November 1817. B.M. Add. MSS. 35, 153, f. 52.

[3] Place to Hodgskin, 8 September 1819. B.M. Add. MSS. 35, 153, f. 73.

taxes and fines. He had sympathised with the sufferings of the "much governed"[1] Germans, and had seen in Germany a typical example of a country where men governed too much, "though from good motives".[2] In his accounts of his travels he found room for all the anecdotes demanded by his publisher to make the work amusing.[3] To a public, which for twenty years had almost forgotten the existence of continental civilisation, he gave an abundance of interesting and novel information about North Germany and, in particular, about Hanover with its English king. But, above all, his description and information were accompanied by a sort of running commentary, consisting of a considered criticism of the ideas of government and law.

For him, to speak of government is to speak of a nation, that is to say of an artificial division, a useless multiplicity of often contradictory regulations. How many governments there are in Germany! And yet everywhere men are alike: why keep them apart by imaginary divisions? "They need but to chase away their different masters to make them all sensible that their interest is everywhere the same." Has one then to pray for the coming of a conqueror who will absorb these many small rival nations into the unity of an empire? Hodgskin rejects this hypothesis. He relies on the general and spontaneous progress of human reason, on the ending of the absurd cult, the "stupid veneration", of great men,

[1] *Travels*, Vol. I, p. 210. [2] *Ibid.*, Vol. I, p. 166.

[3] Hodgskin to Place, 26 July 1819. B.M. Add. MSS. 35, 153, f. 77.

on the imperceptible propagation of the beneficial science "whose truths have been systematized and incorporated into the experience of mankind by Smith, Say, Malthus, Paley and Bentham". He does not want the "square, mechanical" unity which would come with a universal despotism and which would reproduce on a greater scale the vices of the governments which it had superseded.[1] The weakness of a one-man government is a matter of mathematical proof.

> To suppose that, when a whole nation take part in making and examining laws, it will not be better regulated than when laws are made by one person only, is to suppose that the wisdom of the whole race is not equal to the wisdom of the smallest of its parts.[2]

Nor would substituting a parliamentary regime for a dictatorship produce a better order of things. Hodgskin here clearly has adopted the teaching of Godwin. Legislative assemblies, he contends, are not a guarantee of wise legislation. If, for the suppression of a few abuses, a nation were to place a blind reliance in its Parliament, it would be giving itself, purely and simply, a new master. What makes the English constitution so excellent is the existence, not of a House of Commons, but of a watchful public opinion informed by a free press and constantly concerned with checking the activities of Parliament.[3] As this watchfulness begins to wane the House of Commons, too small in numbers to free itself from subjection to the Crown, will reproduce the vices of government by a single individual,

[1] *Travels*, Vol. II, pp. 204–5. [2] *Ibid.*, Vol. II, p. 444.
[3] *Ibid.*, Vol. I, pp. 459 ff.

under the deceptive appearance—sufficient to lull public disquiet—of government for all.[1] In fact, by their very nature, Hodgskin maintains, governments are neither interested in, nor capable of, good government.

To what conclusion then does this lead? From this failure of human wisdom, asserts Hodgskin,

> . . . it is clear that the limits within which the power of government ought to be confined, and beyond which it becomes pernicious, are yet absolutely unknown; and when it is remarked, that the prosperity of every nation is in an inverse proportion to the power and to the interference of its government, we may be almost tempted to believe the common opinion, that governments are necessary and beneficial, is one of those general prejudices which men have inherited from an ignorant and a barbarous age, and which more extensive knowledge and greater civilization will shew to be an error full of evil.[2]

If, indeed, he continues, one accepts the view of Adam Smith that society is subject to the operation of natural and necessary laws, either the directives of positive law will be contrary to, or they will conform with, the commandments of nature. In the first case it is clear that they are harmful: but in the second it may seem that they are merely useless. Actually even in this case they are harmful. For one thing, in practice, the officers appointed to supervise the execution of the laws have to be paid, and this payment upsets the natural harmony of interests. To prevent crime a police force is set up: the wages of the police are paid out of the produce of the labourer: the police force is the more costly because

[1] *Ibid.*, Vol. I, pp. 465–6, 468.

[2] *Ibid.*, Vol. I, p. 417.

the profession is unpopular and because the number of policemen goes on growing. "So the labourer is reduced to poverty; the inequality of his condition is further augmented and this causes more crimes than the best organised police can suppress."[1] Furthermore, to pass from the observation of a law of nature to the promulgation of a penalty against anyone who transgresses it is to maintain a fatal confusion of ideas in the mind of the governed.

The makers of guild laws have erred, as almost all law-makers err, from not distinguishing two things which are in themselves essentially distinct and different. These are, a *desired line of conduct*, and a *law* to compel that line of conduct. It is one thing that a man ought to do a certain thing; it is another . . . to make a law to compel him to do it, or to punish him if he neglect it. It is, for example, much to be desired that bank notes should not be forged; but it is perfectly a distinct thing to make a law that men shall not forge bank notes, or to sentence them to be hung if they are detected in doing so. The effect of this is to encourage a line of conduct directly contrary to that desired. Experience has shewn it; and when men are told they must not do any certain action under the penalty of being hung, they are immediately persuaded that it will be a great advantage to them to do it, provided they can escape detection.[2]

The German governments, Hodgskin says, patronise the arts and sciences: in this they are wrong. Undoubtedly the life of the German universities is preferable to that of the English universities "owing to our rigid adherance to Gothic regulations". The German universities are subject to the capricious directions of the sovereign and his minister, but these

[1] *Travels*, Vol. I, p. 333. [2] *Ibid.*, Vol. II, p. 179–80.

at least, belong to their age and may happen to have an enlightened outlook.[1] On principle, however, for Hodgskin, all state education is of a conservative and traditional character.[2] It is expensive and contrary to the lessons of political economy. In so far as the sciences and arts are useful they are in demand and find the price in the market which is their due; and the very fact that many scholars and artists do not find employment for their talents proves, not that they should be assisted, but that, in these instances, the supply has been made to outrun the demand.[3]

The German governments also patronise industry and control the distribution of landed wealth. But the state nurseries and salt-works which Hodgskin has visited have seemed to him to be only moderately prosperous. The real property laws of Hanover, he recognises, have had good results: they have prevented both the fragmentation and the excessive concentration of estates. But, according to Hodgskin, these evils, against which certain laws might usefully have been enacted, proceed themselves, in the last analysis, from other laws; for the essential function of legislation, the work of the rich, is to protect wealth. "The simple means of making the race frugal is to supply the wants of no man and to leave every man the produce of his own labour. This would be the best Agrarian law which could possibly be made";[4] and Hodgskin, not without some appearance of paradox, opposes to the example of Germany that of England, where "pro-

[1] *Ibid.*, Vol. II, pp. 266–7.
[2] *Ibid.*, Vol. II, p. 258.
[3] *Ibid.*, Vol. II, p. 278.
[4] *Ibid.*, Vol. II, pp. 86–7.

perty in land has been entirely free . . . the owner has been at liberty to dispose of it as he thought fit", and, as a result, "private interest has, in this instance, effected a great public good, without any limitation or direction by the legislator".[1]

The German governments want to prevent poverty by public assistance laws: always there is this same absurd desire to substitute the rules of law for those of nature. Hodgskin, who in other respects had already set himself apart from Malthus, in this matter continued to think like him. Marriage between paupers in Hanover, he says, is subject to the permission of the magistrate. From this it is to be concluded that every marriage which the magistrate authorises is lawful and sacred. Actually, the misery which may follow from a marriage is the natural reason why it should not take place, and "this important fact the magistrate prevents the parties from knowing by substituting his permission for the natural reason".[2] The ruling class—the wealthy class—is conceited enough to believe that it lies in its power to relieve poverty by legislation. But law, the work of the rich, is, by its nature, the cause of poverty. How then can it lessen poverty, except fortuitously?

The landlord and the capitalist produce nothing. Capital is the produce of labour, and profit is nothing but a portion of that produce, uncharitably exacted for permitting the labourer to consume what he has himself produced. When this is given to him as charity, if he be not oppressed, he is at least insulted. Those who imagine themselves to be very benevolent people, while they dole out

[1] *Travels*, Vol. II, p. 95. [2] *Ibid.*, Vol. II, pp. 99–100.

to the labourer a pittance of what they have exacted, delude themselves with a hypocritical cant, that, however it may be sanctioned by laws and however it may accord with the customs of society, was never surpassed by any of the cant of the most absurd religion. By your labour shall ye eat bread is holy wisdom, and he who does not gain what he consumes by his own industry, eats assuredly . . . the bread which nature made the property of another. The poor are the terror of the rich, and the scourges of society. But the affluent have little right to complain when their repose is disturbed, for it is they who inflict poverty on their fellows, and at the same time teach them to desire wealth. The evils of society cannot be remedied by acts of parliament. . . . Generally it seems to be supposed, because the rich make laws, that the poor only need restraints, and to be reformed. This is a mistake. It is the class of society that has long ruled that most needs reformation, and that deserves most of the blame for the social evils which exist.[1]

The fallacy of the Germans is to be found, in the last analysis, in a false conception of political economy, which to them is "the knowledge of promoting the prosperity of the people by means of government",[2] whereas in reality it consists of the knowledge of natural laws, in conforming to which the general interest is achieved without government intervention.[3] From this mistake there follows the attribution to nature of the responsibility for crimes whose real authors are governments and laws. Instead of explaining the existence of crime and misery in terms of an artificial state of society, in which an aristocracy of wealth exercises an influence no less pernicious perhaps than "an aristocracy of

[1] *Ibid.*, Vol. II, pp. 97–8.
[2] *Ibid.*, Vol. I, p. 414.
[3] *Ibid.*, Vol. I, p. 467.

birth",[1] in which "he who produces everything receives almost nothing while those persons who produce nothing revel in superfluity", and in which "industry is the slave of idleness, and, from being constantly associated with poverty and contempt it has become more shunned and abhorred than crime itself",[2] they prefer to attribute all the distress to industry and commerce.

Employing different kinds of labour to supply different wants never can produce poverty and distress. And for the benefit of mankind, in order that no species of industry may be unjustly brought into discredit, those social regulations ought to be exposed to censure, which have inflicted on us so much poverty and distress. All the different kinds of productive labour must be beneficial, but the manner in which its produce is distributed in the society is distinct from the labour itself and is the result of social regulations. From confounding these two things, and from being serious in wishing well to their country, I have heard several clever men in Hannover express a wish that they might not become a commercial people.[3]

But if the existing distribution of property is both unjust and artificial (and for Hodgskin the two things are basically the same), if it is due to the legislative intervention of a "few separate and distinct individuals, acting as a government in the name of the whole",[4] it is illusory to consider the general movement of Europe towards industrial and commercial freedom as anything but an irresistible revolt by the laws of nature against the laws of man. Only those in the existing society have cause for alarm who place

[1] *Travels*, Vol. II, p. 163.
[2] *Ibid.*, Vol. I, p. 302.
[3] *Ibid.*, Vol. II, pp. 111–12.
[4] *Ibid.*, Vol. I, p. 292.

all their happiness in having their wants provided for by unremunerated and trembling slaves. . . . According to their view, morality consists in quietly submitting to misery if it be inflicted according to law, and every attempt which men make to escape from this legitimately inflicted misery is stigmatized as immoral.[1]

Only those who believe in the play of fortuitous forces in history can hope to impede this movement.

The morals of a nation cannot be suddenly changed or destroyed by any single event. . . . No miraculous change ever has, or ever can take place, in the conduct of a whole nation, and he who attributes the immorality of any people to a single event, not only rejects the evidence of a regular government in the moral world, which every day brings before him, but also all the evidence of history. The moral laws of nature are as regular and unalterable as her physical laws. He, who has so beautifully constructed our bodies, has not left our conduct, on which our happiness depends, to be regulated by chance. The power which governs the world is not a sanguinary tyrant, who delights, by momentary and unexpected storms, to blight the best hopes of mankind. Regular laws are established in the moral world, and we have a capacity to discover them, and so to regulate our conduct by them, that we may diminish or destroy every species of evil.[2]

While the *Travels in the North of Germany* was appearing Hodgskin was busy organising his existence in the great intellectual city—proud of its great men, its university, its critical *Reviews*—where for a year he had been living. He had contacts with Constable, the editor of the *Edinburgh Review*, with Napier, the publisher of the *Supplement to the*

[1] *Ibid.*, Vol. II, pp. 462. [2] *Ibid.*, Vol. II, p. 465.

Encyclopaedia Britannica, and with MacCulloch, the chief editor of the *Scotsman*. He was trying to make a living by writing articles for the *Reviews*, expecting his knowledge of German language and civilisation to find him opportunities. At the same time his wife was learning English and trying to give lessons in German. But he also continued to pursue his own lines of inquiry; and at no time was his work more fruitful than this. Utilitarian radicalism was the starting point for his reflections. From the time when he had first had the benefit of Francis Place's advice and patronage, his relationship with the group of Bentham's friends had been close and constant; and, indeed, at every point where the Benthamites defended the cause of liberalism, Hodgskin's radicalism was on all fours with theirs. He was pleased at the progress which the idea of free trade was making in England. He wrote on a House of Lords debate on foreign trade,

> . . . the confessions on both sides, particularly acknowledging our legislation had hitherto been wrong and that when laws were permanent men would conform their conduct to them, appear to me of importance. The first is a confession of insufficiency and the last a proof that men would find *even* the laws of nature convenient if my Lord Liverpool would allow us to follow them. Nothing is more constant than they are, and nothing in the shape of *Laws* can be more changeable than the regulations of both honble. houses.[1]

He applauded the campaign for Free Trade which

[1] Hodgskin to Place, 30 May 1820, B.M. Add. MSS. 35, 153, f. 159 v.

MacCulloch was conducting in the *Edinburgh Review*.[1]

> Undoubtedly the abolition of all restrictions of whatever kind is the great point to be aimed at. We want a destroying legislature whose great business would be to do away the enactments of their predecessors.[2]

He acted as intermediary between MacCulloch, whom he saw regularly, and Place, with whom he was in correspondence, at the time when the former, keeping step with the Westminster Radicals, was beginning to campaign for the repeal of the combination laws.[3] Hodgskin shared the indignation of the Radicals about the prevailing reaction and protested against the Manchester massacre. His only cause for astonishment was to find that the liberal opposition's primary concern was with discovering whether the massacre was a violation of the laws.

> The horrid violation of the laws at Manchester seems only now to be a cry and a watchword to support them. Productive as it has been of miseries, it is our miserable constitution we are now told we must defend and support. I am heartily sick of such a nonsense. I should like to know the single law that is worth an honest man's struggle. This is not the law of Parliament, nor the law of the Judges, nor the laws relative to free trade nor to freedom of speech and writing; in short I do not know one that of itself is worth supporting, but all men seem to think it is better to be sabred by hussars or shut up in Bastilles according to rules than trust their fellow men.

[1] Hodgskin to Place, 23 April 1820, B.M. Add. MSS. 35, 153, f. 137 v.

[2] Hodgskin to Place, 27 August 1819, B.M. Add. MSS. 35, 153, f. 78 v.

[3] Hodgskin to Place, 1 September 1819, B.M. Add. MSS. 35, 153, f. 79.

They seem to think it better to be fleeced according to rule than run the most remote possibility of living according to reason.[1]

In an article which he submitted to the *Scotsman* in January 1820, and which the *Scotsman* refused, Hodgskin developed this idea of the great work achieved by the new philosophers. "Adam Smith, Mr. Malthus, Mr. Bentham and all the political Economists and writers on legislation for this last half century . . . had shown the absurdity of almost every regulation which they had examined and, as necessary consequence, had weakened the respect of all men for the authority from which these absurdities had emanated".[2] But his anarchism went much further than their reformism: he did not attack particular laws but every law without exception or, more precisely, the idea of law itself.

The economic philosophy of the Benthamites, he states, is based on opposition to legislative intervention: why then should it be otherwise with their philosophy of law? That the idea of positive law is absolutely irreconcilable with the existence of natural law was the concept which Hodgskin's mind had seized upon in his earliest reflections and reading. But, if such is the case, how can one explain the existence and origin of positive law? To every law, without qualification, Hodgskin extends the Benthamite explanation of the origin of bad laws or, as they put it, of "sinister" laws. Such laws, he says,

[1] Hodgskin to Place, 2 September 1819, B.M. Add. MSS. 35, 153, f. 82.

[2] Hodgskin to Place, 20 January 1820, B.M. Add. MSS. 35, 153, f. 120 v.

have been made by oligarchies for the defence of their own private interests against the general interest of the people.

Hodgskin thereupon gave up his time to investigations into the origin of laws and asked Place to enlighten him on certain points relating to biblical times.

Were not all the nations of antiquity of which we have any knowledge composed of Masters and Slaves? And may not Penal Laws, or rather did they not, originate in such a state of society and were they not principally intended to keep the slaves in order?[1]

He sent off a request to Francis Place for a copy of Bentham's *Traités de Législation*[2] and managed to get published in Constable's *Magazine* an article on the penal code, very moderate in tone and containing a tribute to Bentham. But a second article, which was to have been a continuation of the first, was rejected.[3] For the time being Hodgskin allowed his interest in this fundamental problem to drop.

On other points, also, Benthamism invited criticism. In questions of constitution law the utilitarian radicals attacked monarchical and aristocratic systems of government, but only to propose in their place a parliamentary democracy in which the harmony of interests of rulers and ruled would be assured by procedures which were to some extent mechanical. Hodgskin, who had already warned the

[1] Hodgskin to Place, 8 February 1820, B.M. Add. MSS. 35, 153, f. 124 v.

[2] 15 February 1820, B.M. Add. MSS. 35, 153, f. 126 v. Cf. 20 April, f. 133.

[3] 15 February 1820, B.M. Add. MSS. 35, 153, f. 129.

readers of his *Travels in Germany* against the superstitious veneration of a representative form of government, was sceptical about the efficacy of this legislative mechanism. At one point he thought of undertaking a critical history of parliamentary legislation in England.[1] Then James Mill published, in Napier's *Supplement*, his famous *Essay on Government*, which defined the constitutional programme of the Benthamites; and Hodgskin, in a letter to Place in which he discussed James Mill's ideas, set against the idea of democratic government that of a society without any government at all. If public opinion is the sole moving force of a constitution, he asked, why should not this same public opinion, without any constitutional mechanism, be sufficient to establish a stable society? Against James Mill he revived the doctrine of Godwin.

He assumes as settled the only question I should be disposed to argue, viz., "that the object of government (the protection of property) is best accomplished when a great number of men combine together and *delegate to a small number the power necessary for protecting them all*". Grant this and the whole train of reasoning is masterly and supplies many new and good arguments against bad Government. But I am disposed not to grant this. Experience tells me that men can associate to protect one another without any delegation of power to a few. Thus the people, at present driven by a common desire, have united for the protection of the Queen and in fact have protected her against the power of a bad Government, without any delegation of power. In a similar way I think it is improperly assumed in the argument against Democracy that the people must be assembled to make laws.

[1] Hodgskin to Place, 20 April 1820, B.M. Add. MSS. 35, 153, f. 133.

In the present state of our society there is no occasion for this. The opinion of every individual on any given subject might be known in a few months without bringing the nation together. And this would be rapid enough for the purpose of making Laws. I am disposed therefore to dissent from Mr. M. in this part of his subject, and to think that as far as "*Legislation*" is concerned "the community in a mass is not ill adapted for the business of government". I think the illustration of the benefit club not quite complete. For a benefit club, I believe, only appoints office-bearers and does not allow them or the committee of management to make *laws*, which is however implied in the usual idea of powers of Government and seems to be included under them by Mr. M. If Legislation is not included under the power to be given to a few, I have scarcely any reason for objecting to the whole, but if it is, then it appears ill founded, because the checks instituted by the whole people, and which are afterwards supposed to make the Government, have the same interests with the people, could assuredly protect the people without the intervention of this Government (or the delegated few) as well as against it or them. Or in fact the checks which suppose a power left in the people of declaring what is right, is, in truth, the essence of Legislation, and not only ought not to be, but appears incapable, while checks are preserved, of being delegated. Preserving the power of Legislating in this one important point of checking the delegated few, I do not see why it should not be preserved in all, or, in other words, that there is any reason why the power of legislation should not be exercised by the whole nation without any delegates whatever. The case is however different with regard to the other two branches, Administration and Judicature. These must be entrusted to delegated individuals, but probably both, nationally considered, should be confined within much narrower and very different limits from what they are at present. I do not pretend to say, however, to what extent; though I should suppose the relations of

Nations to each other, the only occasion on which national administration, such as Kings and Ministers, could be required, would be very few.

Mr. M. seems to have been somewhat misled by not attending to the real source of the powers of Government. They are, of course, nothing distinct from the wealth and privilege which the opinion of people in favour of Government confers on it, or allows it to appropriate to itself. Or *Government* has no power to protect property but what it derives from opinion. If opinion is capable of *constituting*, of restraining and of giving every government particular powers in proportion as opinion varies, I am at a loss to tell why opinion could not, in the first instance, protect property (the end for which Government is instituted) without the intervention of such an operose machine. But I will not say any more on the subject. Grant that the best way of protecting property is for many men to delegate the powers of administration, Judicature and Legislation to a few, assume the fact of Government being necessary from the desire of men to appropriate to themselves the *objects of desire*, and the article is excellent.[1]

But Hodgskin's dissatisfaction with the Benthamites was not only occasioned by their philosophies of penal and of public law: even their economic philosophy failed to satisfy him. While Hodgskin had been travelling in Italy and Germany, the literature of radicalism had been enriched by Ricardo's great work in which he defined anew the doctrine of Adam Smith and gave it added features; but Hodgskin believed he must condemn Ricardo's innovations because he saw in them so many infractions of the great principle of the new philosophy, the principle of the natural harmony of interests.

[1] Hodgskin to Place, 17 September 1820. B.M. Add. MSS. 35, 153, f. 169 ff.

Adam Smith had maintained that, in the world of exchange and of the division of labour, the natural laws of production and distribution are harmonious and beneficent, a natural harmony only to be upset by historical accidents, by the appropriation of land or the accumulation of capital. Then came Malthus, finding a cause for poverty independent of human will in the naturally excessive growth of population and the natural disharmony which exists between the number of consumers and the quantity of food. Rent, levied on the produce of the labourer by the landowner, seemed to him a necessary consequence of the relative unproductiveness and the scarcity of cultivatable land. Now Ricardo had set himself the task of incorporating Malthus' theories into an integrated system of political economy. In the letters which he addressed to Place, himself a neo-Malthusian, Hodgskin protested against Ricardo's system with its Malthusian elements, and demanded a return to the teaching of Adam Smith by their elimination.

At the time when Godwin, after a silence of twenty-five years, was replying to Malthus' work, Hodgskin, in some respects Godwin's disciple, contested, alongside him, the principle of population. Undoubtedly, in the interpretation of history, Hodgskin attached to the growth in the numbers of mankind the same importance as Malthus had done: but Hodgskin's philosophy of history is optimistic instead of pessimistic. If the multiplication of the human race is a natural phenomenon, he declares, it cannot be other than good: it explains, in his opinion, the permanence, not of poverty, but of civilisation itself, and the progress of men in knowledge and happiness. He wrote an article to show

> . . . that mankind had improved in all the virtues of sobriety, mildness, forbearance, forgiveness, etc. etc. that they had improved in knowledge and ingenuity precisely as their number had augmented, that this was a beautiful contrivance of nature to remedy most of the apparent evils of our condition, and that the sayings which we had heard from the Pulpit and from our wiseacres in Parliament, that a multitude of men was a hot bed of vice and that our crimes were owing to no defect in our Government but to our large cities, were only said to make us believe in the efficacy of Priests and of Lord Castlereagh. The paper appeared to me to contain nothing but facts and to present a view of our natural condition which ought to be consolatory to every man. It was however rejected as being too political. I see people are only anxious to say in a pretty manner what others believe. And as I have always troubled myself very little about a pretty manner and have thought differently from what others think, I find I am most unfit for a scribe.[1]

Twice the article was refused. Malthusianism had become one of the dogmas of the Liberal party, not to be refuted in a Whig publication. Hodgskin ended up by sending a summary of his essay to Francis Place with the request that it be submitted to Godwin.[2] This summary contains, in a short and succint form, all Hodgskin's anti-Malthusianism.[3]

On the Moral influence of an increase in the number of Mankind

1*st*. Admitted that Population has a *tendency* to outrun

[1] Hodgskin to Place, 20 January 1820. B.M. Add. MSS. 35, 153, f. 121.

[2] 30 May 1820. B.M. Add. MSS. 35, 153, f. 159.

[3] B.M. Add. MSS. 35, 153, f. 161 ff.

Subsistence, ought we not to attribute the misery this tendency may hitherto have caused rather to the *ignorance* of man that *this* was a law of nature than to the Law itself?

2nd. Mr. Malthus admits that as population has increased in Britain, for example, famine, pestilence, and all the evils which he says thin a population have become less. Compare the sufferings of a savage of New Holland with those of an inhabitant of England. In Turkey 31 people live on each square mile, in England 152. In the former country pestilence and famine are greater than in the latter. It is therefore ignorance, bad government or some other cause which produces famine and death, not an excess of people.

3rd. There is reason to believe that filth and torpor produce disease, and there can be no doubt these would be greater than they are, if hunger did not stimulate to exertion.

4th. When America, in the possession of Indians, is compared to America, in possession of Europeans, or if the former and present condition of the United States are compared, it is evident that not surface of soil but labour and ingenuity produce food. A few miserable Indians starved on an immense continent. A few people acquainted with the knowledge and arts of Europe have gradually increased to a mighty nation, and they have an abundance of food. Ingenuity and knowledge or some moral qualities of men are therefore the principal means of multiplying food.

5th. There must have been a time when the surface of Europe bore the same proportion as to extent to the number of its inhabitants as America does at this day, but there is no period of the history of Europe in which its inhabitants have multiplied so fast as the inhabitants of America. We must look for some other cause, therefore, besides a deficiency of territory—such as bad government promoting ignorance, and ignorance generally—for the slow progress of population in Europe.

6th. It is a matter of fact that, other things being equal, *knowledge* and *ingenuity* and of course the means to produce food (see 4) must be great in proportion as the numbers of mankind are great, and they must increase as mankind increases in numbers. The mechanic arts flourish in crowded England, the fine arts did in crowded Greece.

7th. Desires multiply with the numbers of mankind and with their industry. Compare the savage basking in the sun with a *literary* and *rich* European.

8th. The increase of knowledge attendant on an increase of population accompanied by an increase of morality. Look at the history of Europe, which has increased in morality as the number of its inhabitants has increased: St. Bartholomews—*Bauern Krieg*—war of peasants, etc. etc.

9th. Increase of morality owing to an increase of population. Collision rubs down and tames passions. The weight of the mass gives force to their opinions which subdues the will of every individual.

10th. Civilised man is a totally different being from a savage man and hardly knows anything of the furious passions of the latter. Hence, it is supposed that every passion may be subdued or rather constrained to the level at which *opinion* justifies indulgence.

11th. Conclusion. An increase of population promotes industry, ingenuity, and knowledge, consequently also the means of producing food. The power of the Populating principle may therefore be looked on as the great stimulus to exertion and as the great means of promoting the happiness of the individual and of the Species.

From the Malthusian principle of population is derived the Malthusian law of differential rent. This law implies that the rent of land is not a fictitious monopoly but the necessary consequence of the operation of natural economic laws. As a result it has to be admitted, either that nature is unjust and the function of legislation is to correct its imperfections (Hodgskin's naturalistic optimism precludes his acceptance of this hypothesis) or that the rent of land, and consequently the existence of a landowning aristocracy, is just since it is natural. (The Physiocrats had accepted this but Hodgskin is too much of a democrat to accept it.) The only way of escape from the dilemma for Hodgskin is the rejection of the theory: and that implies the rejection of the entire Ricardian system. For Ricardo, exaggerating Malthus' error, says Hodgskin, not only adopts the theory of differential rent, but bases on it a complete new theory of the distribution of wealth. He makes the law of profit dependent on the law of rent, asserting that the average rate of profit is determined by the profit of the capital employed in cultivating the poorest land, and that profit is condemned to decrease indefinitely by the obligation of mankind to have recourse to the cultivation of increasingly poorer soils. He makes the law of wages in its turn dependent on the law of rent and calls the minimum income necessary for the survival of a worker and his family the natural wage, because he considers it to be kept at this miserable level by the indefinite growth of rent. Hodgskin contests all these supposedly natural laws.

He rejects the law of differential rent. Doubtless, he argues, it is possible to explain the appearance of rent and of a landowning class by differences in soil fertility; but only experiment can prove if this possible explanation conforms with reality. Ricardo and his followers have no time for experiment.

However, according to Hodgskin, if from the rent of existing farms there is deducted this differential element, on which the school of Malthus insists, there will still remain an enormous sum, equal perhaps to that half of the produce of the soil which was demanded from the old sharecroppers. Differential rent, for Hodgskin, is a negligible element in real rent. The rent of land is to be explained by the historical fact that a small number of conquerors, having occupied all the land, were in a position to demand from each and every cultivator a sum to which a limit has only been set by the need to allow the cultivators to live and work.

From this it follows, for Hodgskin, that the Ricardian theory of a natural wage is also false. The first cultivators of the soil of Europe, he says, lived as slaves, but their descendants, freed from slavery, have persisted in the habits of life of their ancestors; they have continued to accept, under the name of a wage, the equivalent of what the master once conceded to the slave. In the final analysis, the supposed natural wage of the Ricardians amounts to nothing more than a servile custom perpetuated by the laws of men.

And, finally, in Hodgskin's eyes, the supposed law of naturally decreasing profits is also false. If nature were not thwarted in its activities, labour, aided by capital, would become increasingly more productive with the advance of human ingenuity and of machinery. If, however, it seems to become less and less productive, that is because the intervention of human legislation masks the working of the natural laws, because, in the world as it is, the worker does not receive the whole produce of his labour but has payments for profit and rent deducted from it. The Ricardian theory of value on this point leads to a confusion of ideas; and Ricardo is wrong in his desire—contrary to the wiser view of Adam Smith—to identify value in exchange with natural price.[1] To get a proper conception of value in exchange, exchange should be considered, argues Hodgskin, not as being between two articles or between abstract values, but as being between the individuals, who are the makers of the articles and of the exchange. In the world of trade as it actually is producers can occupy very different economic positions. Two given individuals provide equal quantities of work; but the one, the owner of land and capital, receives all the produce of his labour while the other, from the produce of an equal quantity of labour, has to make payment to a landowner and a capitalist. Thus the worker, with what represents the final product of his labour, namely his wage, can buy only a part of the value produced by the other at the cost of an equal quantity of labour.

To sum up: according to Hodgskin, for those who engage in trade products are not exchanged in proportion to the amount of productive work put into them, since, if that were the case, the wages paid to labour would always be equal to the product of that labour. Rent and profit are the artificial cause of the raising of prices to the worker; and the poverty of the workers is a result, not of the operation of

[1] Cf. Hodgskin to Place, 29 April 1821. B.M. Add. MSS. 35, 153, f. 198. See also below, Chap. III, p. 136.

natural laws, but of certain positive (i.e. man-made) institutions and historical accidents.

As early as June 1819[1] Hodgskin submitted to Place the plan of a work consisting of critical observations on Ricardo's system, but Francis Place was too much of a Ricardian to do other than dissuade Hodgskin from carrying out this enterprise. Once he had got rid of the anxieties which arose from the publication of his book, however, Hodgskin's attention was again drawn to the problem of rent. He discussed it for the first time in a short note to Place of 20 April 1820,[2] then in a more fully developed letter on the 28th May,[3] a letter which is here reproduced in its entirety. Hitherto unpublished, it shows the precise extent to which Hodgskin's ideas had matured by this time. Well documented and reasoned, in spite of a quick and at times prolix style, it is of interest as much for its contents as for the date of its composition—less than three years after the publication of the *Principles of Political Economy and Taxation*.

I am much obliged my good friend by your long letter of May 23rd, which I received the day before yesterday and which has given me some cause for thinking ever since it came. I do not agree however yet to the doctrine of Rent, and I mean, if you have patience to read through my remarks, to explain at more length my reasons for dissent. I am pleased at having an opportunity of disputing with you because I am sure if I should be conquered in the end the *victory* will be to my own advantage.

I think it is in general ridiculous for a man to speak of

[1] 4 June. B.M. Add. MSS. 35, 153, f. 67.
[2] B.M. Add. MSS. 35, 153, f. 135 v. ff.
[3] B.M. Add. MSS. 35, 153, f. 142 ff.

impartiality, either when he examines or controverts the opinions of any other person. We have all some pre-formed opinions of our own which we like in general better than the opinions of others, and we only approve or condemn these as they are different from or agree with our own. I have therefore no hesitation in saying that I dislike Mr. Ricardo's opinions because they go to justify the present political situation of society, and to set bounds to our hopes of future improvement. They have the first effect by justifying our great Land-Leviathans in their enormous exactions. *Wealth* is but another name for political power, and with an aristocracy of Land-lords such as at present exists anything like democracy is impossible. We are all subjects of Nature, and we can only be either happy or great by obeying her laws. And if Rent, such as it at present exists, be according to Mr. Ricardo the natural result of the progress of Society, then every attempt to rid us of the control of a wealthy aristocracy must be ultimately unsuccessful and in its progress mischievous. I am a *democrat*. Mr. Ricardo's doctrines are the strongest support I know, as far as reasoning goes, to aristocracy, and therefore I dislike them. This is the source of one of my prejudices against them which I thus honestly and openly confess.

Mr. R's opinions set bounds to our hopes for the future progress of mankind in a more definite manner even than the opinions of Mr. Malthus. It is, namely, Mr. Ricardo's opinion that the rate of all profit is ultimately determined by the rate of profit gained by capital employed on land, that this is constantly diminishing by a necessity for having recourse to poorer soils, and that there is a point, limited by the natural interest of capital and from which most European societies are not far removed, at which improvement must stop. I have always supposed from the progress men have hitherto made that it is impossible for us to limit their future progress. Mr. R's doctrines do this exactly and they do it on natural grounds, and because they are thus opposed to this other prejudice of mine, I dislike them very much. Having shewn you the ground of my prejudice against them, I shall attempt to justify it by reasoning and facts.

I do not in the first place deny that there may be a difference in different soils which may make the produce of some greater than others—that the necessity of having recourse to these worse soils has increased rent in modern times—nor that Mr. Ricardo's doctrines do not very happily explain the great increase of Rent within this last half century. But I deny that Rent originated in this difference of soil and that the *Rent* which is now paid is *nothing but* the difference between the produce of equal quantities of capital employed on soils of different powers of production. For Adam Smith said, and he said truly, that men pay a rent for fish ponds, for rivers, for gathering kelp, and for barren moors. Or, what is the same thing, they pay some monopolists for the permission to *fish in rivers*, to gather kelp on the sea shore, or to cultivate what is without labour a barren waste. Undoubtedly a greater Rent is paid for a good soil than a bad one, but what is now *called* Rent is greater than the difference between the produce of good or bad soils by a sum perhaps quite equal to that half of the produce which the former Land-lords of Europe exacted from their slaves.

I have before met with the account of the sands of Norfolk, which you give me, having been made fruitful by labour and now paying a rent, and on this fact, combined with several others of the same kind such as the whole of Holland and the whole plain of Lombardy, both of which like Norfolk have been made fruitful by labour, may be grounded the strongest objections to the whole of Mr. R's theory of Rent and of *natural* profits decreasing in the progress of society. This shews clearly as you say that *some lands* paying rent have no *original* and *indestructible powers*, but I am disposed to extend this to all *land* and to affirm that it is *human labour* which makes any soil productive, and that it is from land-lords having originally monopolised the labour of their slaves that rent is now paid in Europe. We know that the *powers* of the *soil* in North America and New Holland were as nothing till they were called into existence by the labour and ingenuity of Europeans. They did not save the few miserable savages that roamed over immense tracts from the miseries of want. Independent of human labour there is no original indestructible power of the soil. A similar ingenuity to that which made the sands of Norfolk productive has made the swamps of Holland and the gravel of Lombardy productive. And a similar ingenuity might at this moment, could it be done without asking the permission of the kings and monopolising land-lords of Germany, make the whole sands and bogs of Moravia, Prussia and Hanover probably quite as productive as the once loose sands of Norfolk. What are now called the very worst soils may, by some improvements or alterations in the mode of agriculture, be made as productive as what are now called the best. For example, the introduction of sheep has made the highlands of Scotland pay much higher rents than they used to do. But nobody could use any part of the formerly waste territory of my Lord Breadalbain for this purpose without paying him *Rent*. And he would take care to augment this rent whenever the farmer should make so much by the use of the land as to tempt any other person to suggest to *My Lord* that he could get a greater rent for his sand. These improvements shew us that Rent, though it may be augmented by some diversities of soil, was not originally, and is not at present wholly, paid for any indestructible powers of the soil.

You do not say whether you admit the fact of the greater part of Europe having been cultivated by *Slaves* or not. This appears to me in the inquiry to be a fact of primary importance. I have looked therefore at Hume's England, Robertson's Charles the Fifth, Miller's Historical View, Kames' Sketches of Man, Adam Smith, etc., etc., and they all agree that nearly the whole of Europe was formerly cultivated by *bondsmen*. I assume, therefore, as an established fact that all European society was formerly divided into masters or Landlords and slaves. Since this early period another class has grown up, who, possessing capital and ingenuity, have neither all the *authority* of Lords nor are they so abject as the slaves. This class has not originated so much in laws as in the natural progress of society, and it would in time, but for the regulations of government, primogeniture laws, etc., etc., quite absorb the other two, and we should have in the world a democracy of well informed, well provided human beings. Putting this large and increasing class out of the question, we still find in society the descendants of Landlords and the descendants of the slaves. The first are the landed aristocracy, the last are *the labourers* and *handworkers* of society. We know that the aristocracy have always had the *Political* power of the country in their hands and that the "*Statutes for Labourers*" and other laws have always kept the wages of labour at a level nearly with the minimum of subsistence. Hall very pertinently asks, in his travels in Canada and America, if the situation of a slave would be improved by making him free, if he would not be obliged to be contented under the name of a free man, while the masters continued monopolists of the soil, with the smallest measure of subsistence. And in another part of his work he answers this by saying that, where the greater part of a community are in a state of slavery, what is given to the slaves will, should they be set free, become the measure of the wages of their labour as freemen. I hold this to be true and that the wages of labour in European society at present must be considered as the reward given by masters to *slaves*. Here there are three facts connected with one another of great importance as to that sum at present paid under the name of Rent. 1st: The soil of Europe was formerly cultivated by slaves, a great portion of whose produce went to their employers or landlords; 2nd: Such classes of men have always been found in European society; and 3rd: The wages of labour are at present and have always been in Europe determined by the reward formerly given to slaves. It is an undoubted fact that *land*, and with that every means of subsistence, was overrun and monopolised by a few persons in every state of Europe. And their descendants or the persons who have purchased their rights continue to monopolise the land to this day. They compelled the people living within their districts to deliver to them a certain portion of corn, which in the course of time came to be commuted into money and at present forms that sum paid as Rent. That money Rents are merely a commutation for personal services or derived from them I hold to be certain. Suppose that some one bondsman by excessive parsimony or by flattering the vices of his lord should receive from him a portion of his monopolised land, he would in truth receive some part of his lord's power over the labour of the rest of the slaves who dwelt within the district he had received, or his lord would give him at least his own freedom and produce. Suppose a man, by trade, by going abroad, by any other circumstances, acquired a considerable capital and on return to his native country he was enabled to purchase from one of these land-monopolists a part of his estate, would he not purchase from him the power which this monopoly gives over the labour of the bondman who dwelt on the estate? And if he, not having the privileges of *noble birth*, could not possess all the power which this circumstance gave to his predecessor, should release the *bondmen* of personal service, would they not *still*, all the rest of the land being monopolised, be obliged to work for him on his own terms or starve? And if he afterwards let any large portion of his land, would not the sum paid to him under the name of rent be in reality paid for a share of his privilege of exacting a portion of the labour of the bondmen? Suppose a Scotch farmer—a thing which has in truth happened—was to hire of some Polish or Russian nobleman a track of land, with all his ingenuity he could cultivate by his own labour but a very small portion, but by the help of the labours of the peasants which the lord would grant him at the rate of 6d. a day a head, he might cultivate a whole county, and the rent he would then be enabled to pay would be much more in proportion to the number of people he employed compared with their absolute produce than to the extent of surface his labours were spread over. And in either letting or selling him such a track of country the nobleman would in truth sell or let him not the original and *indestructible power* of the soil, but his power over the labour of the slaves who dwelt on it. The origin of that Rent which is at present paid is this. Some few men conquered others and monopolised the whole soil of the country. At first they employed and fed their slaves and appropriated to themselves the produce of their labour. They afterwards sold or exchanged this power over their slaves to other persons who released the slaves from personal service but still compelled them to labour on the terms of Landlords. It is for a portion of this *power* over an *already appropriated* land that rent is paid in Europe. It cannot be positively affirmed but I am disposed to believe such a thing as Rent would never have existed had there never been *Slaves*. No argument can be drawn against this supposition from the state of North America because a large portion of the *labourers* of that country are the descendants of the slaves of Europe and are nearly as much dependent on those who already possess soil and capital as if living in Europe. America, in truth, suffers as well as Europe from the vices of the early state of society in the latter country as much as she benefits of what was good in its knowledge and institutions.

If Mr. R's account of the origin of rent be true and it never amounts to more than the difference between the produce of good and bad land, then Rent can never enhance Price. He has got over all the difficulties of this part of the subject by his, I think illiberal, definition of the price of labour. Adam Smith was much more just. Mr. R. has found labour rewarded in our society as if the labourer were a slave and he has assumed this as his natural condition. If the origin which I have ascribed to Rent be correct, it enhances the price of every thing and impedes our progress by bringing wastes and other lands which are at present uncultivated under the plough, not only by the sum which it is requisite to pay Landlords for permission to cultivate these wastes but also by enhancing, to the persons who could cultivate them, the price of every thing they consume while their produce is becoming fit for consumption.

Mr. R. has involved this part of the subject in considerable confusion by *supposing* the buyers or the community who pay prices are different from the three great classes, to wit landlords, capitalists and labourers, among whom he divides the produce of the earth. For all political-economical purposes however it seems right to consider the whole community as composed of these three classes, and, though Adam Smith has not uniformly adhered to this division, yet in all which he says on the subject of Rent and profits increasing prices he evidently supposes the society to be composed of these three classes. In fact both he and Mr. Ricardo make the *real natural price* of all things to be paid by *labour*, and it is therefore self-evident that whatever diminishes the *value* of labour or makes a greater quantity necessary to obtain an equal quantity of any commodity enhances *its price*. All price is paid by labour. Now Rent is a part of the produce of labour, taken by a person who does not labour, and, of course, if the labourer wishes to obtain for his own use a quantity of produce equal to the quantity obtained which he has shared with the *lord*, he must double, treble and in the present day must multiply his labour manyfold to obtain it. Rent, therefore, enhances price, by the whole of amount of Rent. Profit, being in like manner a diminution to the labourer of the value of his produce, enhances the price of everything into which it enters to the labourer. It is in this sense in which A. Smith says rent and profit enhance price, and considers the whole produce to be divided into these and wages or among the three classes mentioned. No truth in the whole course of reason was ever more self-evident. It is abundantly clear that rent and profit cannot enhance the quantity of labour necessary to obtain any commodity from nature, but they enhance its price to the labourer by their whole sum. In proportion therefore, as Rent and Profits increase, the reward of labour will gradually decrease; the price the labourer must pay for commodities will gradually increase. So that, whenever high Rents and large capitals on which great profits are paid exist, the labourer will never have more than what is barely necessary to support existence. And I am afraid, my good Friend, we may look in vain for any permanent amelioration in the political condition of Society while the industrious part of it, the payers of all natural price, they who buy everything from nature with their toil, are condemned to hopeless poverty and degradation, and while the price of every thing is so enormously high to them that they can procure but the very smallest portion. Rent and profit do not enter into price if Mr. Ricardo's account of the origin of the former be true and if it is supposed that *buyers* are other than labourers, if they are capitalists or landlords for example. They do, however, and constitute the greatest part of it, if the origin I have ascribed to Rent be correct, and if the buyers are to be considered as labourers and not capitalists or Landlords. I hold this manner of considering buyers as either distinct from these classes, or as *labourers*, to be the ground of the difference in the opinions of A. Smith and Mr. Ricardo on the subject of rent and profits not entering into *price*. Another source of this difference seems to be, the want of an accurate distinction between *natural price* and *exchangeable value*. Natural price is measured by the quantity of labour necessary to produce any commodity: its exchangeable value, or what another will give or is obliged to give for this commodity when produced, may or may not be equal to the quantity of labour employed in its production. Mr. Ricardo has, I think, made a mistake by supposing these two things to be equal. They are not, or the wages of labour would always be equal to the produce of labour. It requires for example a certain portion of labour to produce a quarter of corn. This quarter of corn, however, when produced and in possession of a man who is at the same time both landlord and farmer will, at present, exchange for a prodigious deal greater quantity of labour than it cost to produce it. There is therefore a great difference *between* real natural price and exchangeable value, and by not attending to this Mr. R. has been led into—I think—great mistakes relative to the decrease of profit in an improving state of society.

I have before stated his opinion on this subject, and you will see how perfectly unfounded it is, if you reflect for one moment on the *real natural price* of raw produce at present and *its real natural* price one or two centuries ago, that is the quantity of labour now and formerly necessary to obtain any commodity from nature. By improvements in agriculture and machinery there can be no question that less labour is required to produce equal quantities of corn in England or any land now under tillage than was required two or three centuries ago. It is not only as machinery and ingenuity have been directly applied to agriculture that the cost of production has been decreased, but as its application in a thousand ways have diminished the cost of production of all those instruments and commodities which either aid production or are consumed by the labourer while he is employed in the work of production. Thus the improvements which enable men to make ploughs, stockings, cloth cheap, or to bring articles of food cheaper from a foreign country, enable the people engaged in the work of production to produce at a less cost, because what they consume while they are producing costs less. That this is the true state of the case is proved by the fact that the productive labourers at present maintain a host of unproductive labourers of every species, when in the early stages of society every man was obliged to work to obtain wherewithal to live. In other words, any quantity of capital now employed in the work of production is repaid many fold more than an equal quantity of capital was several centuries ago, or, where the labour of a savage scarcely produces him enough for subsistence, the labour of an intelligent European peasant maintains at least 12 persons. Natural profits of capital can only mean the value which results from employing it in the work of production. And if it be true that a greater value results from capital employed at present in the work of production, or that it returns greater value than an equal quantity of capital employed in the same work three centuries ago, then have the natural profits of capital increased and we may hope they will go on increasing. I hold it to be a clear fact that raw produce is now obtained in our country for a less natural price, or at a less expence of human labour, than it is in *Poland* or than it was in our country some centuries ago, or what is the advantage of what we call improvements? Its exchangeable value, however, augmented as I am disposed to contend by the whole amount of Rent and profits, is greater in Britain than in Poland. Mr. R. appears to me to have confounded in the whole of his speculations real natural price with exchangeable value. The former is accurately measured by the quantity of *labour* necessary to obtain any commodity from nature, the latter on the contrary is the quantity of labour augmented by the amount of Rent and profits. The real natural price of a quarter of corn is all the labour, whether of the men who make ploughs or carts, or till the ground, or any other necessary to its production. Its exchangeable value must however be so great as to pay the profits of all the capital and all the rent paid on any of the articles which are, in any way, employed in its production. If we regard *labour* as the measure of *natural price*, we see at once how vastly the augmenting and continually augmenting ingenuity of mankind has diminished and is continually diminishing—in direct opposition to the theory of Mr. R.—the natural price of every commodity. Capital can only be considered as machines, food, etc., and, in as much as the capital employed or consumed by an ingenious and industrious man produces more than the capital consumed or employed by an ignorant or idle man, in so much must the *Capital* of the ingenious and industrious inhabitants of modern Europe be returned to them with a greater increase than the capital of ignorant and lazy barbarians. The natural profits, therefore, of capital constantly increase with the ingenuity of our species. Labour and ingenuity, much more than the powers of the soil, produce food; and at least ingenuity, and I am also disposed to believe industry, augments with the increasing number of mankind. Unless, therefore, some limitation can be set to our increase in knowledge and ingenuity, it is impossible to limit the natural profits of capital on the production of food.

I am aware that Mr. R's doctrines suppose no restrictions, but he supposes the present rents, except in so far as they are increased by our own restrictions on importation of corn, as the natural and just ones. Of course the prohibition augments rents, but the sum they would sink to, if there were no prohibition or monopoly whatever, would still assuredly be much greater than the mere difference in value between the produce of the worst and best soils in cultivation. Mr. R. has settled it in his own mind that the *natural price* of *labour* is what saves the labourer from starving (see def. Chap. 5), that profits of capital are nearly equal in all employments—which is true—and he then regards *rent* as the sum remaining when the wages of the slave *labourer* and the profit of the capitalist are paid. This is modern rent, but it is somewhat more than the difference of the produce of good and bad soils. I think I never saw a book more destitute of facts than Mr. R's, which, at the same time, has had so much weight. To me it appears to rest entirely on arbitrary definitions and strange assumptions. The two first sentences of the book[1] are radically false. The circumstances there ascribed will undoubtedly have a wonderful influence on the whole quantity of produce, but the manner in which it is distributed will depend entirely and exclusively on political regulations. No circumstances of *soil*, *capital* nor ingenuity will ever make the distribution of wealth the same in the United States of America in which slavery is unknown [*sic*] and in our Empire of India. This definition of value is wrong. Labour is the measure of price, and though exchangeable value can never be lower than equal to the payment of the labourer, it may be and is higher than this in almost every conceivable degree. According to his own definition the *indestructible powers* of the soil, which are not labour, have a very considerable exchangeable *value* in the hands of *monopolists*. His explanation of the manner in which fixed capital tends to lower the prices of all commodities into which it enters I hold to be the best and only good part of his book.[2] He cannot deny that taxation enhances *price*, and yet according to his definition it ought not, for it does not, any more than rent or tythes, augment the quantity of labour necessary to bring raw produce to the market. I may have read his book prejudiced against it. I believe I have; but, after making every allowance for my prejudices, it does appear to be built on no sort of facts, to contradict many and to have little more merit than a "bewildering subtlety".

You do not agree with Mr. R. as to value—but I do not understand exactly what you mean by the use of capital.[3] I should like to know this. Profits do not increase the labour necessary to bring a commodity to the market, but they enhance its price to the labourer and its exchangeable value to any person not a capitalist.

[1] Evidently the first two sentences of the preface in which the distribution necessary between the three classes—landowners, capitalists and workers—is treated.

[2] *Principles*, Chap. I, Sect. iv.

[3] Allusion to a letter of Place which we do not possess.

And there can be no doubt that the quantity of capital in the society and the manner in which it is distributed will have a decided influence on exchangeable value. I believe with you that there could be such a circumstance as one man gaining more from a good than another from a bad soil and thus enjoying *rent* but, though this circumstance might have made such a race as Landlords, I contend that those who now exist are the inheritors of a power over slaves, not the mere possessors of a more fertile spot. In looking at Robertson's *America*, I see it stated that a portion of the Produce of the mines was set apart for the king. This is rent. All the mines of Europe and all the precious metal were originally claimed by the Sovereign, and nobody could either work them or pick up money without paying them. Rent therefore is paid on all precious metal. If you suppose that some more productive mines or some better way of working a particular mine is discovered, then a second rent may arise to the proprietor or worker. The metals gained from all the mines will continue to pay rent to the king, but he who owns the richest mine or who has discovered the easiest method of obtaining metal—supposing always that the whole quantity is only equal to the demand—will also have a rent; or a sum will remain in his possession greater than that in the possession of the workers of other mines. This is also precisely the case with corn land, and in short, with all raw produce. A rent either in corn or money was paid by the labourer to the lord for all land which was capable of being laboured. Favourable situation, however, fruitful land, new inventions in agriculture, added a second, a third and even a fourth rent to the original demand of the lord. The latter may be just and might have arisen from the very nature of the soil, the first, however, which is probably the largest, is unjust and is the result of slavery.

Thus Hodgskin was the first to uncover the real incoherence of the doctrine of those followers of

Bentham who so ostentatiously set themselves up as precise logicians. At one point they maintained that the harmony of interests is achieved by the operation of the laws of nature; at another, they saw, as the function of positive law, the realisation of this harmony. In the political economy of the utilitarians Hodgskin found again the same contradiction between the optimism of Adam Smith and the pessimism of Ricardo. The strength with which he believed, with Adam Smith, in political economy, in the existence of natural laws, at once beneficient and harmonious, was the moving force which made him determined to criticise the supposedly natural laws of Ricardo as soon as he had seen in them the causes of poverty and disharmony. For the time being his heaviest criticism was directed against the role assigned by Ricardo to land in the production of wealth and the place which he gave to the rent of land in its distribution. On capital and profit he was less clear. He seems to have believed in the existence of a "natural profit", and to have concluded, on the basis of the growth in the output of labour, that there was a growth in the productivity of capital. Already, however, he regarded rent and profit as two indistinguishable results of a single historical cause, namely of what may be called, in Marxist terminology, the separation of the worker and the means of production. Already, in his *Travels in Germany*, he would appear to have put together, under the single name of profit, the return to both the capitalist and the landowner; and in his letters written from Amsterdam to Francis Place he had already begun to apply those same methods of analysis to the

Ricardian theories of capital and profit, which he applied in 1820 to the theory of differential rent.

Meanwhile life became hard and work difficult. His book did not bring him in a penny; the Reviews did not want his articles; his wife and he were no longer able to find pupils. He thought of translating foreign books, Malte-Brun's *Geography*, a *History of Prussia*, a *History of the Hanse*; but for these he needed a publisher. He thought of librarianship but for that he would have to know Greek. Finally, his wife fell ill[1] and while she was convalescing at her father-in-law's in Deptford, Hodgskin lived on his own in Edinburgh, becoming increasingly gloomy and dispirited. For a long time, from London, Place had been plying him with exhortations and good advice, reproaching him for his over-discreetness and timidity. "I know a little German . . .", Hodgskin had written. Why, answered Place, do you disparage yourself so? You know a great deal of German: turn your knowledge to good account. "I lead a hermit's life", wrote Hodgskin. And that, answered Place, is just what you must not do. "If I had power over you, you should lead a dog's life by way of punishment; you would soon find reason enough to choose better. Why, man, if I had led a hermit's life I should now have been a journeyman breeches-maker starving in a garret or a cellar, or the workhouse. Go you into the world as much as you possibly can, and learn of it something every day."[2] However, Hodgskin continued

[1] Hodgskin to Place, 4 January 1822. B.M. Add. MSS. 35, 153, f. 203.

[2] 8 September 1819. B.M. Add. MSS. 35, 153, f. 73.

in his self-chosen isolation, despised by all, Whigs as well as Tories, journalists as well as parliamentarians. But journalism was in the end to provide him with a livelihood. Place suggested that he should come to London to try his hand at parliamentary reporting (doubtless on the *Morning Chronicle*, whose publisher, Black, was the friend of James Mill). As a result of this suggestion Hodgskin set himself to practise listening to sermons and university lectures with a view to editing them from his notes.[1] In his own estimation he had little success and he became more discouraged. Furthermore he knew no Latin; how would he manage when orators quoted from the classics? His letters to Place daily became more full of anxiety and despair. He neither could nor would remain in Edinburgh; he was afraid that, if he were left there, he would lose "all spirit and every capability of exerting himself".[2] Mrs. Hodgskin was writing equally disturbing letters to Place from Deptford. She was afraid for her husband's state of mind; she could not endure the life she was leading in her father-in-law's house.[3] Finally, through James Mill, Hodgskin obtained, on the *Morning Chronicle*, the situation which he wanted. At the end of 1822 or the beginning of 1823 he arrived in London; he had been lifted out of his poverty.

[1] 28 March 1822. B.M. Add. MSS. 35, 153, f. 204.
[2] 15 April 1822. B.M. Add. MSS. 35, 153, f. 207.
[3] 2 and 9 May 1822. B.M. Add. MSS. 35, 153, ff. 209, 210, 211.

CHAPTER TWO

1823 – 1832

The Mechanics' Magazine – The Mechanics' Institute – *Labour Defended against the Claims of Capital* (1825) – *Popular Political Economy* (1827) – *The Natural and Artificial Right of Property Contrasted* (1832)

In 1824 Parliament, by a memorable law, granted the right of combination to British workers. But Hodgskin, who was present as a reporter at all the debates of the Commons, had no illusions about the nature of parliamentary liberalism in those days of successive reforms.[1] Each time that it appeared to be granting a new liberty to the British people, Parliament was only disguising beneath a pompous ceremonial its obligation to yield to the irresistible pressure of public opinion. In the debate on the legislation of 1824 it was the followers of Bentham and Ricardo who undertook the mission of translating the aspirations and demands of that opinion into a precise form, but they themselves were driven forward by a proletariat who relied on the new law and the combinations, which it allowed, to eliminate the capitalists and restore to the workers, individually and collectively, the enjoyment of the

[1] *Nat. and Art. Rights of Property*, p. 110.

fruits of their labour. From 1823 Hodgskin, resisting the absorbing demands which his journalistic work made upon him, was among the most active in enlightening, instructing, and in organising the agitation of the workers.

In the first months of his stay in London Hodgskin joined forces with one, Robertson, in the establishment of a weekly review, designed to present scientific knowledge in a popular form and addressed to the mechanics, the factory workers. His associate, who had also recently come from Edinburgh, was a man of doubtful reputation, but intelligent and active. Their review, the first of its kind, aimed at providing the reader every week with "Accounts of all new Discoveries, Inventions and Improvements, with illustrative Drawings, Explanations of Secret Processes, Economical Receipts, Practical Applications of Mineralogy and Chemistry; Plans and Suggestions for the Abridgment of Labour, Reports of the State of the Arts in this and other Countries; Memoirs, and occasionally Portraits, of eminent Mechanics". Parliament was just preparing to repeal the old laws which fixed the wages of silk-workers in the Spitalfields industry. Hodgskin, who supported the repeal, opened an inquiry on this subject in the second number of the *Mechanics' Magazine*. His secret wish was to prove to the discontented silkworkers of Spitalfields that their economic condition in this protected branch of industry was worse than that of workers in unprotected industries. The *Magazine* therefore invited its friends to furnish information about the average wage and weekly hours of work in the different towns in which they lived. For it was evident, stated the *Magazine*, that the English worker was overworked.

The reason why there is no work for one half of our people is that the other half work twice as much as they ought. The markets of the world are overstocked with the produce of their industry. It is a maxim with political economists, that products always create their own market; but this maxim is derived from the supposition that no man produces but with the intention of selling or enjoying, and it does not therefore hold good with our labourers who are compelled to produce but are not permitted to enjoy. Theirs is an Egyptian bondage.[1]

In a second article, the *Magazine* warned the workers, who asked for legal protection, against their illusion about the effect of law. In the case of the Spitalfields silk-works all that the magistrates had done was to give legal sanction to the prevailing price of labour, a singularly low wage of seventeen shillings a week where the working day was twelve or fourteen hours. Moreover, it continued,

legislators have always belonged to the *non-labouring* classes of society, and it seems bad, therefore, for the poor man to have any law of this kind emanating from them. The individuals of these classes are already too powerful for him, and a law which is, and always will be, we are assured, the expression of their combined will, merely adds to their power. Even supposing the effect of the law might be to keep wages from falling, if it be not for the interest of the labourer to work at a lower rate, he must already be sadly degraded, when he needs a regulation, enforced by penalties on the part of his master, to prevent his injuring himself.[2]

[1] *Mechanics' Magazine*, 6 September 1823.
[2] *Ibid.*, 4 October 1823.

At the end of this article, a third was announced which was to continue the discussion of the problem. But the promised article did not appear: a new enterprise was taking up all the energy of Robertson and Hodgskin.

At Glasgow some workers had come together and had formed an institute on a permanent basis in which they employed teachers of science and technology. In Edinburgh and Liverpool similar institutions had been set up. If this type of establishment had prospered in the North, could it not be acclimatised to London? Could not the teaching of the printed newspaper be supplemented by the oral instruction of the lecture, the *Mechanics' Magazine* by the Mechanics' Institute? Such was the new idea of Robertson and Hodgskin. On 11 October, in the *Magazine*, Hodgskin launched an appeal to the public. For their technical education the English workers must do, through their own efforts, what the state had already done in France and Austria.

The education of a free people, like their property, will always be directed more beneficially for them when it is in their own hands. When government interferes, it directs its efforts more to make people obedient and docile than wise and happy. It devises to control the thoughts, and fashion even the minds of its subjects; and to give into its hands the power of educating the people is the widest possible extension of that most pernicious practice which has so long desolated society, of allowing one or a few men to direct the actions, and control the conduct of millions. Men had better be without education—properly so called, for nature of herself teaches us many valuable truths—than be educated by their rulers; for then education is but the mere breaking in of the steer to the yoke; the mere discipline of a hunting dog, which, by dint of severity, is made to forego the strongest impulse of nature, and instead of devouring his prey, to hasten with it to the feet of his master.

The workers of London should follow the example of the workers of Glasgow and found, at their own expense, a new institution where they might learn everything that it was now indispensable for a worker to know in chemistry, mechanics and in the science of the production and distribution of wealth.

The London Mechanics' Institute was established; but, to ensure the success of the enterprise, Hodgskin approached his friend and benefactor, Francis Place, the universal organiser. Place quickly explained to Hodgskin and Robertson the impossibility of founding a stable institution simply on the subscriptions of working men; he overcame their opposition and obtained their consent to opening a subscription list along with all the notable members of the radical group.

But it was not without regret that Hodgskin and Robertson gave up their ideal of a purely popular institution. No doubt they also realised that, with every important figure who lent his support to the institution, their own influence would further diminish. An obstinate struggle took place between Hodgskin and Robertson, on the one hand, and Francis Place, on the other, especially from the time when Dr. Birkbeck lent a large sum on interest to found the institution. Was this working-class enterprise to become a source of revenue for a capitalist?

Place carried the day. He could hardly have failed to do so; for he was a former workman, now become employer, with experience of life and knowledge of men, and with a talent for methodical organisation and for well-ordered accountancy, while they were writers, journalists and the most irregular of book-keepers. Though provisional secretaries of the Mechanics' Institute, Robertson and Hodgskin were not elected on 15 December 1823 as members of the administrative commission; they were replaced by a paid secretary, and the Institute of which they were the true originators slipped from their control.[1]

The breach between Hodgskin and the Benthamites cannot, however, have been complete if it is true, as a family tradition maintains, that Thomas accompanied Bentham, as secretary, on the latter's triumphal journey to Paris in September 1825. In any case he did not break with the Mechanics' Institute which he needed for the propagation of his ideas. From October 1823 he had before him the aim of planning a course of instruction in political economy directed to a working-class audience. In 1824, when the opportuneness of repealing the laws restricting freedom of combination was under discussion, he was shocked by the weakness of the arguments put forward by the workers against those of the capitalists. While the Ricardians were endeavouring to show that freedom of combination did not bring about either reduction of profits or migration of capital, no one was denying the argument that the elimination of profits and the transformation

[1] For this entire episode, see Place's unpublished MSS., *Early history of the London Mechanics' Institution.* B.M. Add. MSS. 27, 823, f. 240 ff., and *Mechanics' Magazine*, *passim.*, and particularly No. 199, 16 June 1827.

into wages of the whole produce of industry would mean either the ruin or the diminution of national industry. In a curious pamphlet written in 1821 Piercy Ravenstone had tried to make plain the illusions of the political economy of capitalism;[1] and Hodgskin, to strengthen the working-class cause,

[1] *A few doubts as to the correctness of some opinions generally entertained on the subjects of Population and Political Economy*, London, 1821. Piercy Ravenstone wishes to show that "whenever the numbers of a people increase more rapidly than its means of subsistence, the fault is not in Providence, but in the regulations of society" (p. 23). He defines the right of property in similar fashion to Hodgskin: "He who has killed the bear appears clearly to be entitled to his skin" (p. 197). He gives a similar explanation to Hodgskin of the social deformation which has overtaken the right of property. In origin "the land was looked upon as belonging to him who had first rendered it useful and whose industry had first given it a value. . . . Its possession was looked upon as only the just reward of his industry. This species of property is, however, very different from that artificial right, which grows up in the progress of society, by which a man is enabled to appropriate to himself the ownership of lands which he does not occupy, and on which he has never exercised any industry. A right which enables him to live in plenty, without any labour of his own, and to exact from others a large portion of the fruits of their industry, for the permission which must be derived from him to employ their labour in rendering productive lands, in which all appear to have an equal right of property. This pretension of the landowner is, indeed, the basis of the property of every description, which is seen to multiply so rapidly with the growth of civilization. On it are built the pretensions of the master-manufacturer, of the tradesman, of the capitalists" (pp. 199–200). From this point labour ceases to be free; rent and profit end by absorbing almost the whole produce of labour: "the fund for the maintenance of the idle is the surplus produce of the labour of the industrious" (p. 233). There follows a criticism of the concept of capital from which Hodgskin has borrowed extensively. "It is not a very easy matter, however, to acquire an accurate idea of the nature of capital. It is quite another sort of being from its confederates. Rent and taxes have an avowed

took up Ravenstone's thesis and completed and amended it in his *Labour defended against the claims of capital*, which was published in 1825 by the editors of the *Mechanics' Magazine*. To propagate this criticism of the Ricardian theory of production, he relied on the Mechanics' Institutes.

No Holy Alliance can put down the quiet insurrection by which knowledge will subvert whatever is not founded in justice and truth. . . . They may care nothing about the curious researches of the geologist or the elaborate classification of the botanist, but they will assuredly

existence. . . . But it is not so with capital. It has none but a metaphysical existence. . . . Its treasures are not real wealth, they are only the representations of wealth. They may be increased to any imaginable amount without adding to the real riches of a nation. Capital is like the subtle ether of the older philosophers. . . . It is no less useful to our economists than that was to the philosophers. It serves to account for whatever cannot be accounted for in any other way. . . . It is the deity of their idolatory which they have set up to worship in the high places of the Lord" (p. 293). There follows a rather complex theory of profit, conceived as being exacted by the tradesman from the worker. "Both rent and profit, both property and capital equally arise from the surplus produce of the cultivator's labour. The one cannot acquire an unnatural increase without proving injurious to the claims of the other. The only difference between them is, that one shares directly, the other indirectly, in the earnings of the productive labourer." Capital is not a factor of production: it is either to be classed with the tradesman's stock—which is not dependent on the tradesman for its existence—or with machines —which are produced by labour and have no economic existence except through the application of labour—or with the accumulation of profits—"here we immediately see that capital is only the transfer of property from one person to another" (p. 346). It is not the emigration of capital but that of poor workers which is to be feared. In a final chapter, called *Political consequences of the distribution of property*, Ravenstone sees in the maldistribution of property the basic cause of crime.

ascertain *why* they only of all classes of society have always been involved in poverty and distress.[1]

In the event, he soon broke with Robertson, left the editorial staff of the *Mechanics' Magazine*, and, by a singular turn of events, became the close associate of Birkbeck. "The friend of Dr. Birkbeck", "the Doctor's man",[2] such were the ironical expressions which were loaded upon Hodgskin by the *Mechanics' Magazine*. At the Institute he requested, and in 1825 obtained, permission to give a course in political economy. Francis Place, influential as ever, protested and the experiment was not repeated. Two new series of lectures dealt with the philosophy of history and with psychology.[3] But the lectures of 1825,[4] developed and re-emphasised, became in 1827 the first volume of a *Popular Political Economy*;[5] that is to say, political economy not vulgar-

[1] *Labour Defended*, p. 31.

[2] *Mechanics' Magazine*, 12 December 1829.

[3] Place to Birkbeck, 11 June 1825. B.M. Add. MSS. 27, 823, f. 369. Hodgskin gave a series of lectures in September and October 1826 (*Mechanics' Magazine*, 25 November 1826) and another, "On Mind", in January 1828 (*Mechanics' Magazine*, 9 February 1828). He gave in all three courses (*Daily News*, 27 October 1856), On *Political Economy*, on *General Grammar* and on *The Progress of Society* (*Daily News*, 14 January 1859).

[4] [The original has 1815 but this is clearly a misprint.—*Translator*.]

[5] *Popular Political Economy, from lectures delivered at the London Mechanics' Institution*, by Thomas Hodgskin, formerly honorary secretary to the Institution. London, 1827. The titles of the four lectures were (*Pop. Pol. Ec.*, p. xvii): The Influence of Knowledge; Division of Labour; Trade; Money and Prices. The chapters of the book are: Introduction. Object and Scope of Political Economy. Book I. Natural circumstances which influence the productive power of labour. Chapter I—Mental and

ised and written down to the level of a popular audience, but conceived from the standpoint of the interest of the people[1]—a working class, or, as one might say today, a proletarian political economy.

As in his letters to Place seven years before, he here demands a return to Adam Smith. By contrast with J.-B. Say and later writers, he refuses to include consumption in the number of subjects with which political economy is concerned.[2] He criticises the new conception of economics as an abstract science dealing with the measurement of value. He even protests against the name currently applied to this branch of knowledge. Adam Smith, he says, did not give the name of political economy to his investigations into the production and distribution of wealth: on the contrary he criticised the existing systems of political economy, "showing in fact, that the science which pretended, under this name, to add to the wealth of the people through the instrumentality of government, had and could have no existence".[3] Finally, much more precisely than

bodily labour. Productive labour. Chapter II—Influence of observation and knowledge. Chapter III—Natural laws which regulate the progress of society and knowledge. Chapter IV—Influence of the division of labour. Chapter V—Causes which give rise to, and limit, division of labour. Chapter VI—Territorial division of labour. Limit to division of labour from the nature of employments. Chapter VII—Trade. Chapter VIII—Money. Chapter IX—Prices. Chapter X—Effects of the accumulation of capital.

[1] *Pop. Pol. Ec.*, p. xix.

[2] *Ibid.*, p. 6.

[3] *Ibid.*, p. 43. Cf. p. 3. Cf. *Economist*, 12 December 1846, p. 1622.

the school of Ricardo, Adam Smith was able to distinguish, among "the circumstances which influence the productive power of labour and determine the distribution of goods", two sets of causes. Firstly, *natural circumstances*

> . . . laws not dependent on, or derived from government,—such as the passions and faculties of man, the laws of his animal existence,—and the relations between him and the external world.[1]

These, says Hodgskin, are not the work of man, whose only concern is to avoid violating them, an aim which he may well attain; for these laws, shown by statistics to be regular and "as permanent and verifiable as any other laws of the material world", can be an object of scientific investigation. Secondly, *social regulations*,

> . . . depending on, or originating with governments,—such as those permanent laws which appropriate the soil of a country, or which bestow on it a constitution establishing a diversity of ranks among its inhabitants; as well as the laws for the regulation of trade and the acts of the Administration, . . .[2]

But,

> . . . there can be no science of the regulations of any one government, or of all governments, for they vary, according to no discoverable rule, both of themselves and in relation to the ever altering circumstances of the people, for whom they are made. There may be a science of the natural principles by which legislators ought to regulate their conduct, but there can be no science of their decrees.[3]

To distinguish between the natural laws and the social conventions, or, more exactly, to prevent the

[1] *Ibid.*, p. 23. [2] *Ibid.*, p. 23. [3] *Ibid.*, p. 36.

recognition, as essential factors of production or as natural forms of distribution, of purely accidental forms of distribution, was the task which, according to Hodgskin, still remained to be accomplished in political economy after Ricardo's work.

In land, capital and labour, it is tempting to see three independent factors of production. But is it true, in the first place, that land is a source of the wealth of nations? In his *Labour defended* Hodgskin invokes the theory of differential rent (to be criticised by him so severely five years later) to save himself from the necessity of examining the question of land.[1] Has not James Mill made the observation that this theory amounts to a proof that the rent of land is not an element in the cost of production? Yet the theory of differential rent itself implies that land has a natural fertility and that this fertility varies with climate, geographical position and the nature of the soil: it implies that the natural resources of the soil give an advantage to some at the expense of others. In his *Popular Political Economy* Hodgskin strives, as far as he is able, to reduce the importance of these natural advantages. Has not one seen a nation with an unchanging soil and climate pass from the lowest stages of poverty to the highest condition of prosperity, and *vice versa*? Think of the history of North America and of the empires of Asia: on the same land the productive power of individuals has undergone tremendous variations. From this it must be concluded

> . . . that we may at once reject from our inquiries all the physical circumstances, and all material things not inherent

[1] *Lab. Def.*, p. 6.

in man himself, and not created by labour, which are supposed in general to influence most strongly the prosperity of our race. Climate and situation, however apparently influential, have in reality so slight a degree of power and their peculiar effects depend on causes so little known to us, that at present they are inappreciable. . . . The land falls not within the limits of the science any more than the sea or the air. . . . I do not assert, that what we call fertility in soils, which is in all cases, however, a quality relative to our knowledge at the moment we speak, has no influence whatever on the quantity of labour necessary to procure subsistence; but that influence is so unimportant, compared to the effects of knowledge-guided labour, that it may be neglected.[1]

But then, if labour is the only source of value, how is the fact that land has a value in exchange to be explained?[2] Hodgskin cannot clear up this apparent paradox until, on a second point, he has rid the theory of natural production of the foreign elements with which it is encumbered, and has discussed the part played by capital along with land in the production of wealth. In both cases the fallacy of ordinary political economy is for him the same. It confuses a state of civilisation which is artificial and deeply disturbed with the natural social order. From the fact that, in the existing state of society, the landowner draws a rent from his land and the capitalist a profit from his capital the political economists conclude that rent is the natural produce of land and profit the natural produce of capital.

. . . shutting out of view MAN himself, in order to justify the existing order of society, which is founded on property

[1] *Pop. Pol. Ec.*, pp. 15, 16, 19.

[2] *Ibid.*, p. 4.

or possessions, and the existing oppression of the labourer, who forms unhappily part of these possessions—all these glorious effects have been attributed . . . to fixed and circulating capital. The skill and the art of the labourer have been overlooked and he has been vilified; while the work of his hands has been worshipped.[1]

Before Hodgskin, Piercy Ravenstone had tried to dissipate this illusion, this "fetish", as Marx was to call it, and Hodgskin in his turn writes:

One is almost tempted to believe that capital is a sort of cabalistic word, like Church or State, or any other of those general terms which are invented by those who fleece the rest of mankind to conceal the hand that shears them. It is a sort of idol before which men are called upon to prostrate themselves, while the cunning priest from behind the altar, profaning the God whom he pretends to serve, . . . puts forth his hand to receive and appropriate the offerings which he calls for in the name of religion.[2]

It is the destruction of this idol, the criticism ot this verbal illusion, twice undertaken in *Labour defended* and in *Popular Political Economy*, which constitutes the fundamental thesis of Hodgskin's economic doctrine.

The economists since the time of Adam Smith had made a distinction between fixed and circulating capital. MacCulloch in the Supplement of the *Encyclopaedia Britannica* had just revised the definition. Circulating capital, for him, comprises "all foodstuffs and other commodities applicable to human subsistence", fixed capital "all the instruments, the machines which assist or might assist production". Hodgskin accepts this double defini-

[1] *Lab. Def.*, p. 19. [2] *Ibid.*, pp. 16–19.

tion and contends that profit cannot express the real productivity of this thing which is asserted to be capital, whether fixed or circulating.

The workman, in the course of his work and before its product is forthcoming, he argues, has need of subsistence. Has there to exist, therefore, at the outset, a tangible fund of circulating capital, of provisions accumulated in advance, for the labourer's subsistence?[1] So the economists have been led to think. But all their reasoning has been based on this premise, inspired by analogies drawn from agrarian conditions, that "what is *annually* produced is *annually* consumed". Thus, the produce of each harvest is the capital which for a year will be the means of existence for the labourers, the sowers, the reapers of the next harvest, and so on *ad infinitum*. But such is not the case in practice. Many economic cycles have a more rapid course: though the cultivators gain the product of their work in a year, they eat their bread from day to day; and the baker bakes the bread from day to day, counting on being reimbursed for his daily advances from the yearly product of the cultivator's labour. Conversely there exists a great number of economic activities whose completion requires more—and much more—than one year: to the worker who is engaged in these the producer of corn and wine advances the yearly product of his labour in anticipation of the day when he will be paid in full for his annual harvests from the produce of less immediately productive labours. The fact that the capitalist, in order to be ready to pay his workers, has to accumulate a certain amount

[1] *Lab. Def.*, p. 8 ff. *Pop. Pol. Ec.*, p. 247 ff.

of cash has perhaps tended to strengthen the illusion. But the real wages of the worker consist not of the actual money he receives, but of what he buys with it: and has not the introduction of paper-money tended to dissipate this illusion which the existence of capital in the form of cash has created?

> . . . when paper-money and parchment securities were invented,—when the possessor of nothing but such a piece of parchment received an annual revenue in pieces of paper with which he obtained whatever was necessary for his own use or consumption, and not giving away all the pieces of paper, was richer at the end of the year than at the beginning, or was entitled next year to receive a still greater number of pieces of paper, obtaining a still greater command over the produce of labour, it became evident to demonstration that capital was not any thing saved; and that the individual capitalist did not grow rich by an actual and material saving, but by doing something which enabled him, according to some conventional usage, to obtain more of the produce of other men's labour.[1]

To sum up: what then is meant by saying of a man that he possesses circulating capital? Simply that he has the power to command the labour of some other man. Furthermore, what is the origin of this power? How has he become aware of it? Without thought, simply by habit.

> As we expect that the sun will rise to-morrow, so we also expect that men in all time to come will be actuated by the same motives as they have been in times past. If we push our inquiries still further, all that we can learn is, that there are other men in existence who are preparing those things we need, while we are preparing those which they need. The conviction may, perhaps, ultimately be traced

[1] *Pop. Pol. Ec.*, p. 248.

then to our knowledge that other men exist and labour, but never to any conviction or knowledge that there is a stored-up stock of commodities.[1]

Other men work while I work; this "co-existing labour"[2] is the real cause of the results which are attributed, under the name of circulating capital, to an accumulation of matter.

There remains fixed capital:[3] tools, machines, buildings, so many necessary ingredients of production whose material reality seems undeniable. Hodgskin, in his *Popular Political Economy*, in which he lays emphasis principally on this second form of capital, recognises that fixed capital provides the capitalist thesis with its most substantial argument. But there are, he says, two things which have to be considered. In the first place, this capital is the produce of earlier work. How is it possible from this to consider—except as an absurdity—that capital is both the result and the cause of labour, both the product and the determinant (*limite*) of industry? Undoubtedly the worker, who has made the tool, the machine or the house, deserves a wage: but the hypothesis is that he has already received it, and that the profit of the capitalist is exacted by the capitalist on top of this wage. Undoubtedly, too, the inventor of the instrument of production deserves a reward. But how rarely does he get it! And what a disproportion there is between the reward which the inventor actually draws and the regular and constant profits which accrue to capital once it has been created. Secondly, fixed capital only produces the

[1] *Lab. Def.*, p. 11. [2] *Ibid.*, pp. 8, 33.
[3] *Ibid.*, p. 14 ff.; *Pop. Pol. Ec.*, p. 244 ff.

value exacted by the capitalist under the name of profit to the extent to which it is employed by present labour. Profit, says the apologist of capital, is the reward for saving: but if fixed capital, once created, is allowed to remain stored idly away, it will slowly go to waste, and, in the meantime, yield nothing. Saving is only productive if it means the advancing of capital—by loan or gift—to a worker who will make use of it. This worker certainly deserves a wage; but this wage does not constitute the profit of the capital whose justification is being sought. A road is an item of fixed capital and needs, for its repair, repeated advances of circulating capital.

But neither the circulating nor the fixed capital return any profit to the road-makers unless there are persons to travel over the road or make a further use of their labour. The road facilitates the progress of the traveller, and just in proportion as people do travel over it, so does the labour which has been employed on the road become productive and useful. One easily comprehends why both these species of labour should be paid—why the road-maker should receive some of the benefits accruing only to the road-user; but I do not comprehend why all these benefits should go to the road itself and be appropriated by a set of persons who neither make nor use it, under the name of profit for their capital.[1]

Is it not sufficient, moreover, asks Hodgskin, in understanding how feeble are the current apologies for capitalism, to state that it is desired that the two forms of capital should be rewarded at the same rate in spite of the differing functions which they perform—the productive industry of a country varying

[1] *Lab. Def.*, pp. 16–17.

according to the *quantity* of its circulating capital and the *quality* of its fixed capital?

To say that there is in wages, and in instruments, a similar productive power, because the capitalist obtains a profit on both, seems to me a blunder of no ordinary magnitude. Had it been intentionally made, it would have been deserving our severest reprobation; for its effect is to justify the appropriation by the capitalist of that large share he now receives of the annual produce. It ascribes to *his property* merely, whether he employ it to pay wages, or whether it consist in useful instruments, all that vast assistance, which knowledge and skill, when realized in machinery, give to labour.[1]

To his *property*; that is to say, to the privilege, given him by the laws of the society to which he belongs, of deducting a portion of the produce of labour. How can it be concluded, except absurdly, from the fact that profits and wages are separated from one another, and that the profits, so deducted, come to constitute a fund of capital by being accumulated, that capital plays a part in the production of wealth? The theory of the existing distribution of wealth, considered as natural by the Ricardians, needs revision.

As in 1820, Hodgskin here defines the supposedly natural wage of the Ricardians as the quantity of products necessary for the maintenance of a slave. Nature, to provide man with a given object, demands from him a certain quantity of labour—the real or natural price of the object. The capitalist, to surrender the same object to the worker, demands from him, in addition to the quantity exacted by nature, a still greater quantity of labour.

[1] *Pop. Pol. Ec.*, pp. 249–50. Cf. *Lab. Def.*, pp. 19–20.

The labourers do only receive, and ever have only received, as much as will subsist them, the landlords receive the surplus produce of the more fertile soils, and all the rest of the whole produce of labour in this and in every country goes to the capitalist under the name of profit for the use of his capital.[1]

The demands of capitalism falsify the natural laws of production: they set a fixed limit to wages, whatever the productivity of labour, and as a result set no limit to the growth of profits (since the Ricardians are right in saying that profits and wages vary in an inverse ratio to one another). At present the worker pays sixpence for a loaf of bread with which he would be supplied by nature for a penny. If free trade is instituted, profits will rise and that is all.

Whether there are Corn Laws or not, the capitalist must allow the labourer to subsist, and as long as his claims are granted and acted on he will never allow him to do more. In other words, the labourer will always have to give much about the same quantity of labour to the capitalist for a loaf, whether that loaf be the produce of one hour's or one day's labour. Knowing the vast influence capitalists have in society, one is not surprised at the anathemas which have of late been hurled against the Corn Laws, nor at the silence which has been preserved with respect to their more mighty and, to the labourer, more mischievous exactions.[2]

It is wrong, asserts Hodgskin, to speak of a natural law of declining profits. There is no natural profit: how can there then be a natural law of profits? What is true is that the demands of the capitalists are unlimited. (Remember Price's calculation in which he works out the fantastic sum which a penny,

[1] *Lab. Def.*, p. 6.

[2] *Ibid.*, p. 22.

invested at 5 per cent on the day of Christ's birth, would yield at the end of eighteen centuries.) These claims, being unbounded, should necessarily be held in check by nature: for in the last resort the capitalists must clearly allow the workers, on whom they live, to live themselves. This limit, which nature imposes on the accumulation of profits, is what capitalists call the decline in profits.

In any case, neither the poverty of the workers nor the supposed fall in profits ought to be attributed to the progressive and inevitable enrichment of the owners of the soil. The capitalists deceive the public when they try to mislead them about the respective positions of the landowners and of themselves. The capitalists are the stronger. After taking from the workers all of the produce of their labour which is not essential for their subsistence, they equalise the profits among themselves by leaving to the landowners differences of profit due to differences in the fertility of the soil.

Hodgskin, therefore, returns to the definition of rent proposed by Ricardo. This does not necessarily imply that a revolution has taken place in his thinking since 1820. He would still claim, as in 1820, that the landowner, at the time of the first appropriation of the soil, took away all the surplus as rent; but subsequently, with the progress of movable wealth, all of the produce of labour which does not go to the worker has tended to become profit, except for the differential residue, that remaining part of the booty, which constitutes an excellent contemporary definition of rent. Between the landowner and the capitalist there has occurred a reversal of positions unforeseen by Ricardo's political economy. Under the existing order (as Hodgskin was to write some years later)

all the wealth of society goes first into the possession of the capitalist, and even most of the land has been purchased by him; he pays the landowner his rent, the labourer his wages, the tax and the tithe gatherer their claims, and keeps a large, indeed the largest, and a continually augmenting share, of the annual produce of labour for himself. The capitalist may now be said to be the first owner of all the wealth of the community.[1]

The capitalists further deceive the public, Hodgskin contends, when they maintain a confusion between the profit of capital and the salary due to management in industry. This salary is justified. Though manual workers have too often failed to recognise its legitimacy, the capitalists, for their part, have set it at a higher level than is justifiable: for, on the one hand, mental and physical work are equally necessary to production and, on the other, physical work in itself implies the existence of a mental element whose importance increases with the progress of industry. There is here a double prejudice which will be dissipated by the natural progress of enlightenment, a prejudice which

makes it, and will long make it, difficult even for labourers themselves to apportion with justice the social reward or wages of each individual labourer. No statesman can accomplish this, nor ought the labourers to allow any statesman to interfere in it. The labour is theirs, the

[1] *Nat. and Art. Right of Property*, p. 98. Quoted by Marx, *Capital*, II, pp. 774–5 (First English Edn., 1887).

produce ought to be theirs, and they alone ought to decide how much each deserves of the produce of all.[1]

What is essential is that, through institutions of popular education, the artisans should work incessantly to strengthen the intellectual element in labour; that they should devote themselves—as is fitting in the age of machinery—to lessening the gap separating physical from mental work; and that then, joined together in trade unions, they should succeed in lowering the profits of the employer to the point at which they represent the just wage for his work as overseer and director.

To sum up: the capitalists deceive the public in wishing to see in poverty, which is the consequence of the appropriation of profits, the normal operation of the laws of nature. Population grows without limit; the quantity of available land is absolutely limited; how, in these conditions, will poverty be avoided? Here was the foundation of Malthusian pessimism; but, as we know, Hodgskin stood out for an optimistic interpretation of the principle of population.

As the world grows older, and as men increase and multiply, there is a constant, natural, and necessary tendency to an increase in their knowledge, and consequently in their productive power.[2]

The necessary and sufficient condition for progress in wealth and happiness is to be found, according to Hodgskin, in the division of labour: whatever certain economists may say, it cannot have immoral or

[1] *Lab. Def.*, p. 26.

[2] *Pop. Pol. Ec.*, p. 95. Cf. pp. 125–6. Quoted by Marx, *Capital*, Vol. I, p. 345. (The italics are Hodgskin's.)

degrading effects. Is there less degradation in the work of the labourer in the fields, who is perhaps alone in completing a product without the assistance of others, than in that of the pin-maker?

The dependence complained of and mourned over, therefore, is the dependence of poverty and slavery, and not the mutual dependence occasioned by division of labour. . . . We are thus compelled to fix our attention on the other cause mentioned by M. Storch, and to affirm, that not a part, but the whole of the poverty which he and others have attributed to division of labour, is caused by "*vexatious regulations*". As far as I see my way in this complicated question, I should say that division of labour is an admirable means by which each person may *know* all things; while to enable him to subsist, he is required to perform only one small part of social production.[1]

But what are the causes of the division of labour? They are, firstly, science and the invention of machinery—and science advances in proportion to the growth of population in a given area and the consequent multiplication in the exchange of ideas between individuals; and, secondly, the size of the market—but the size of the market is determined by the number of individuals who demand the product; in other words, in a natural society, it is the number of workers.

. . . the commodity produced by one labourer, the shoes for example, constitutes in reality and ultimately, the market for the commodities produced by other labourers; and they and their productions are mutually the market for one another. But all commodities being the produce of labour, must be plentiful as labourers are multiplied,

[1] *Ibid.*, pp. 138–9. The pessimistic passage borrowed by Marx (*Capital*, Vol. I, p. 348) from *Labour Defended*, p. 25, runs the risk of falsifying Hodgskin's thinking.

or as their productive power increases. The extent of the market, therefore, means the number of labourers, or their productive power; and rather the former than the latter, because the wants of each one are circumscribed, and unless they were to increase in number, there would be neither motive nor means for augmenting production. If this be a correct view of the phrase "extent of the market", we remove at once to an indefinite distance, this limit to the division of labour. It is co-extensive with the number of labourers communicating with each other, and to that number it is impossible for us to foresee or to state any conceivable bounds.[1]

If the size of the market limits the division of labour, this can only be in a society where the rich provide the sole effective demand for the products, where an artificial distribution of wealth lessens the purchasing power of the workers, and where the workers are too poor to buy the products, while the rich are too small in number to consume them. In this sense capital, or more precisely capitalism, places a limit upon industry.

But put the capitalist, the oppressive middleman, who eats up the produce of labour and prevents the labourer from knowing on what *natural* laws his existence and happiness depend, out of view—put aside those social regulations by which they who produce all are allowed to own little or nothing—and it is plain that CAPITAL, or the POWER TO EMPLOY LABOUR, and CO-EXISTING LABOUR are ONE; and that PRODUCTIVE CAPITAL and SKILLED LABOUR are also ONE; consequently capital and a labouring population are precisely synonymous.[2]

The cause of poverty, therefore, is artificial, not natural.

[1] *Pop. Pol. Ec.*, p. 116.

[2] *Lab. Def.*, p. 33.

. . . accumulation of capital in the present state of society checks production, and consequently checks the progress of population, the division of labour, the increase of knowledge, and of national wealth.[1]

In brief, to summarise Hodgskin's theory of production: neither land nor capital are factors of production; the productivity of labour is in direct proportion to the number, activity, and intelligence of the workers—"all wealth is produced by labour".

Now, it seems evident, says Hodgskin, that this natural law of production implies a natural law of the distribution of wealth. While economic theory, which assigns a part to the land in the production of wealth, engenders the spirit of conquest and usurpation, the natural law of production, on the contrary, is

the only safe basis, however, on which the legislator can establish a right of property—if he be at all called on to establish what exists naturally; as it is not only the source of all wealth, but the guide to just distribution.[2]

What is this natural law of distribution? That same law which Ricardo has formulated:

. . . different quantities of labour are *naturally* necessary to procure, and different degrees of difficulty are *naturally* met with in procuring all commodities, and these different quantities of labour, these different degrees of difficulty, establish in our minds a natural relation of value between all commodities, including the precious metals, which, though it may vary, exists at all times and places, quite independent of any human laws whatever.[3]

Hodgskin, more logical than Ricardo's disciples, only adds:

[1] *Pop. Pol. Ec.*, p. 246. [2] *Ibid.*, p. 20. [3] *Ibid.*, p. 186.

The reasoning would be wrong, certainly, if I were to include labour, the creator of all wealth, as they most erroneously do, under the term commodities.[1]

But, like the orthodox economists, and in opposition to the opinion of those who in England at this time were following Attwood's example and recommending the institution of a symbolic currency, he considers the invention and choice of metallic currency as conforming to the laws of nature and as implying no kind of injustice. With the orthodox economists, and in opposition to Robert Owen, he regards commercial profit also as legitimate.

Even in Mr. Owen's establishments, in which retail dealers are regarded as an evil, and rejected as a nuisance, there must be some persons to take care of the food and clothing, and distribute it among the inhabitants of his parallelograms, or the members of his co-operative communities. Retail dealers, therefore, perform such offices for society at large, as quartermasters perform for soldiers, and pursers for sailors, and which somebody must perform for Mr. Owen's pupils. They are not appointed to this office except by nature, but they are quite as useful as if they acted under the direction of Mr. Owen, or by the King's warrant.[2]

No doubt the commissioners under Owen's system receive a salary, while the merchants take a profit: but, says Hodgskin, "were they paid by a salary or wages, what interest would they have in taking care of the common stock?"

Moreover, just at this time, Ricardo's two disciples, James Mill and MacCulloch, were also attempting to establish an identity between capital

[1] Quoted, in a paraphrase, by Marx, *Capital*, Vol. I, p. 547.
[2] *Pop. Pol. Ec.*, pp. 150–1.

and labour. Profit, for them, is an element in value; therefore it is the wage of labour; and therefore it is just. Profit, replies Hodgskin, is a part of value, subtracted by the capitalist from the producer of the value; therefore this part of value, which it is desired should become profit, only becomes such in ceasing to be the wage of labour; therefore profit is unjust. One must distinguish, reply MacCulloch and James Mill, between two forms of labour—immediate and accumulated: profit is the wage of accumulated labour. But, answers Hodgskin in his turn, if capital is to be defined as accumulated labour, it is then not a material mass, a stock laid aside in a store, but is instead this acquired skill, this infused knowledge with which skilled labour is imbued. Of all the productive operations the most important is certainly the education of youth, the teaching of the arts of production; and, adds Hodgskin,

I am particularly desirous of directing the reader's attention to this *productive operation*, because. . . all the effects usually attributed to accumulation of circulating capital are derived from the *accumulation and storing up of skilled labour;* and because this most important operation is performed, as far as the great mass of the labourers is concerned, without any *circulating capital* whatever.[1]

Thus even when they wish to justify profit, the Ricardians admit, more or less confusedly, that, since all value is produced by labour, all revenue is its natural reward. It is the common foundation of their theories and of Hodgskin's. Hodgskin, in a

[1] *Lab. Def.*, p. 13. Cf. *Pop. Pol. Ec.*, p. 125: "Easy labour is transmitted skill." (Quoted by Marx, *Capital*, Vol. I, p. 331.) [Halévy's reference in *Pop. Pol. Ec.*, is erroneous, but I have been unable to trace the correct source of the quotation.—*Translator*].

word, is brought as close to Ricardo as he is to Malthus, and, just as his philosophy of history is a kind of optimistic Malthusianism, so his political economy is an equalitarian Ricardianism.

However, if the natural law of production points the way to a natural law of distribution, the two laws are none the less distinct; and Hodgskin was not content, as the followers of Adam Smith had too often allowed themselves to be, to consider the natural law of distribution, the definition of justice, as a self-evident proposition requiring no justification.

When we have settled the question, however, as to the claims of capital or labour, we shall have proceeded only one step towards ascertaining what ought now to be the wages of labour. The other parts of the inquiry will, I trust, be entered into by some of my fellow-labourers, . . .[1]

And William Thompson, in 1827, in his *Labour Rewarded*, which appeared preceded by an epigraph borrowed from Hodgskin, tried to carry out the programme outlined by him. In his *Popular Political Economy* Hodgskin warned his readers again that he would not deal with the security of property.

Of the former [security of property], which must be considered as an object to be attained by social regulations —though property itself, or a man's right to the free use of his own mind and limbs, and to appropriate whatever he creates by his own labour, is the result of natural laws —I shall not say one word; because it is necessary, before we discuss the effects of security of property, to have the right of property accurately defined, and we must be quite agreed as to its basis.[2]

[1] *Lab. Def.*, p. 5.

[2] *Pop. Pol. Ec.*, p. 236.

Hodgskin thus found himself led back by his economic speculations, a mere incident in the history of his thought, to the fundamental problem which had preoccupied him for more than fifteen years. He again took up his investigations into the philosophy of law, into the essence of natural law and the relationship of natural to positive law. In 1829, when Brougham, seeking the reform of the legal system, had made himself the interpreter in Parliament of Bentham's philosophy, Hodgskin answered him in a series of open letters which contain, alongside a criticism of the Benthamite theory of right, his own theory of natural right. He did not publish them at once; but two years later the Society for the Diffusion of Useful Knowledge devoted one of its pamphlets of economic popularisation to the refutation of the "dangerous" theories of *Labour Defended* and *Popular Political Economy*. The pamphlet was written by Charles Knight: Hodgskin attributed it to Brougham, the director of the Society and the man whose influence at the Mechanics' Institute he detested. He wrote an open letter to Lord Brougham, the Lord Chancellor of England, and published it with the others to establish, in the words of the title, "the contrast between the artificial and natural rights of property",[1] and to formulate, in opposition to the doctrine of Bentham and James

[1] *The Natural and Artificial Right of Property contrasted, a series of letters, addressed without permission to H. Brougham, Esq., M.P., F.R.S. (now Lord Chancellor).* By the author of *Labour Defended against the claims of Capital.* London, 1832. Letter I—Introductory. Letter II—The natural right of property illustrated. Letter III—The legal right of property. Letter IV—On the right of property in land. Letter V—The legal right of property

Mill, the original philosophy of right on which he founded his heterodox and anarchist radicalism. This appeared at the very moment when the orthodox radicals were seeing the triumph of their propaganda in the Reform Act of 1832.

All social theory rests on a philosophical basis; and the true philosophy, according to Hodgskin, is that realism whose tradition has been maintained by English thinkers since the seventeenth century.

> It seems to me that the leading principles of Lord Bacon's, and of Mr. Locke's philosophy . . . that "man is but the interpreter of Nature", and that "all our knowledge of the external world is obtained by means of our senses", or, "is a copy of that world", though these principles have been overlooked by writers on legislation and on the progress of civilization, throw a clear and steady light on many social phenomena. The deductions we may draw from them . . . will prove that the legislator neither could, nor did originate and establish, or even modify to any extent, a right of property. Like the philosopher, he is at best but an incorrect interpreter of a part of Nature. . . . In strict conformity with the great principles taught by Bacon and Locke, I affirm that law-makers only set the seal of their authority to the rights established, or the wrongs practised, by mankind.[1]

This cardinal idea in the philosophy of Bacon and Locke, says Hodgskin, has already been applied by the economists to the interpretation of social phenomena, and Dugald Stewart, the professor and friend

in undergoing subversion by the natural right of property. Letter VI—The law-maker does not establish rights—he only copies usages. Letter VII—Real guarantee of the right of property. Letter VIII—Evils of the artificial right of property. Postscript—To Lord Brougham and Vaux, Lord High Chancellor of England.

[1] *Nat. and Art. Right of Property*, p. 106.

of Brougham, has himself with great preciseness set the statesman the task of finding out "what form of society is fully in accord with nature and justice", and "to what change in the social order do human affairs spontaneously tend".[1] Why then must parliamentary legislators still misunderstand these truths, whose fecundity has been recognised, not only in philosophy, but even in political economy? Why must they abolish certain laws only to set up new ones, instead of recognising the existence of a natural right independent of their decrees? Why must Bentham and the faithful, among them Brougham himself, favour the illusion of legislation and not condemn existing laws except in order to substitute for them a complete new code conforming to their own system?

Let us consider in particular the right of property, whose importance in political economy Hodgskin is here affirming and which, according to its legal constitution, he believes, so profoundly modifies the distribution of wealth.[2] "The Westminster philosophers",[3] those who legislate in Parliament and follow the teaching of Bentham, want government to create the right of property. Bentham in his *Traités de Législation* and James Mill in the *Essay on Government* refuse to admit the existence of natural rights. Before the existence of laws, they assert, it might be useful, and appear desirable, that rights should exist: but it is law which later gives these rights a real existence. Hodgskin condemns categorically this way of comprehending the idea of law.

[1] *Nat. and Art. Right of Property*, p. 4.
[2] *Ibid.*, p. 12.
[3] *Ibid.*, pp. 16–21.

Messrs. Bentham and Mill, both being eager to exercise the power of legislation, represent it as a beneficient deity which curbs one's naturally evil passions and desires (they adopting the doctrine of the priests, that the desires and passions of man are naturally evil)—which checks ambition, sees justice done, and encourages virtue. Delightful characteristics! which have the single fault of being contradicted by every page of history. . . . If the principle be true in one case it must be universally true; and, according to it, parents had no right to the love and respect of their offspring, and infants no right to draw nourishment from the breasts of their mothers, until the legislator—foreseeing, fore-calculating the immense advantages to the human race of establishing the long list of rights and duties . . . had established them by his decrees. . . . To me, this system appears as mischievous as it is absurd. The doctrines accord too well with the practice of law-givers. . . . They lift legislation beyond our reach, and secure it from censure. Man, having naturally no rights, may be experimented on, imprisoned, expatriated or even exterminated, as the legislator pleases. . . . Filmer's doctrine of the divine right of kings was rational benevolence, compared to the monstrous assertion that "all right is factitious, and only exists by the will of the law-maker". [Quoted from Mills' article on Jurisprudence: *Supp. to Ency. Brit.*][1]

Locke's philosophy, says Hodgskin, was very different.[2] According to Locke, mind is the reflection of matter. Clearly, therefore, law, the product of the mind, can record the existence of natural right: it cannot conceivably be considered as creating that right. Nature gives every man the power to work; it gives to each piece of work its reward; it thus creates the right—the natural, not the legal right—of property.

[1] *Ibid.*, pp. 19, 20, 21.

[2] *Ibid.*, p. 61.

> Nature, not the legislator, creates man with these wants, and conjoins with them the power to gratify them. The unpleasant feeling of hunger may be properly called a command or admonition to labour. Nature gives also to each individual: and her separate gifts—as, for example, the fish she bestows on him who baits a hook and watches the line—can no more be confounded with those she gives to another, than the distinct and separate wants they are intended to gratify.[1]

Psychology shows us how we become aware, first of our physical individuality which is our first possession; then how "we readily spread [this awareness] from our hands and other limbs, to the things the hands seize, or fashion, or create, or the legs hunt down and overtake", and to the non-material consequences of our acts; for "in fact the material objects are only sought after for the immaterial pleasure they bestow".[2] And if God or nature—"I use these terms as one", writes Hodgskin[3]—has established the right of property on this basis, he has provided man, at the same time, with the necessary means to defend it. On the one hand, "the same strength or skill which enables one man to catch more game or fish, or create more wealth, than his less skilful or weaker compatriot, will enable him to defend his acquisitions";[4] on the other, "Nature creates the majority of individuals nearly equal in strength, skill and capacity, and gives to all nearly the same facilities for acquiring knowledge":[5] so that it will always be more difficult for a man to take by force from another what the other has already produced than to produce this object for his own use.

[1] *Nat. and Art. Right of Property*, p. 27. [2] *Ibid.*, p. 29.
[3] *Ibid.*, p. 30. [4] *Ibid.*, pp. 30–1. [5] *Ibid.*, p. 30.

The new discoveries of political economy, says Hodgskin, have strengthened Locke's thesis. The important place occupied by the numerical growth of population in the history of civilisation has been recognised. Among its consequences, this growth has the effect of continually increasing the respect for the natural right of property so that, as the face of society changes, natural right itself also changes.

As mankind are multiplied, the moral influence of the mass increases over individuals, and each one, feeling the impossibility of resisting a great many, is humbly submissive to the general voice, and therefore prone to respect that right of property, which is acknowledged by all.[1]

Locke's theory makes justification of the ownership of land difficult; but, as has been shown,

there is no other wealth in the world but what is created by labour, and by it continually renewed. This principle, now universally acknowledged, makes the right of property appear more absolute and definite than it was in Mr. Locke's comprehension, because the right to own land is in fact only the right to own what agricultural or other labour produces.[2]

One might ask, finally, whether the law would continue to hold good in a civilised society where no individual could complete the manufacture of an article on his own. But it appears that it would remain true, if it is considered that

. . . the mutual shares of any two persons engaged in producing one article, as for example, cotton-cloth, is settled by contract or bargain between them, the weaver buying the yarn from the spinner, as the spinner buys the raw material from the merchant importer. If any question

[1] *Ibid.*, p. 40. [2] *Ibid.*, p. 36.

be raised, as to the share of any two or more workmen engaged in the same work, or as to their wages respectively, I shall answer, that this too must be settled by the parties themselves, and is not now in any case the subject of legal enactment.[1]

Hodgskin declares expressly that he rejects the communism of Robert Owen, of the followers of Saint-Simon and of the Moravians; he considers it as contrary to experience and condemned by nature itself. If he criticises the right of property as it is at present constituted, it is only in order the better to defend natural ownership.

The use of such things, like the making of them, must be individual, not common, selfish, not general. . . . It is the right of each individual to own for his separate and selfish use whatever he can make.[2]

To wish to have recourse to the law to define ownership is to make, he says,

. . . an improper intervention between our ideas of individuality, and those natural results of a man's conduct, which are its ordered and appropriate rewards or punishments. . . . As nature gives to labour whatever it produces—as we extend the idea of personal individuality to what is produced by every individual—not merely is a right of property established by nature, we see also that she takes means to make known the existence of that right. It is as impossible for men not to have a notion of a right of property, as it is for them to want the idea of personal identity. When either is totally absent man is insane.[3]

Nature, one might say, is individualistic and individualism is, in Hodgskin's eyes, of divine or natural institution.

[1] *Nat. and Art. Right of Property*, p. 35 note.

[2] *Ibid.*, pp. 35, 41.

[3] *Ibid.*, pp. 30, 42.

If, moreover, Hodgskin contends, laws are considered in their essence and origin, their impotence to promote or to favour the general good will be evident. The legislator claims to be working "to maintain social order, to promote the public good". But "the public good is unknown to human faculties". The social order, "the reciprocal defender of all those who contribute to the subsistence and well-being of society", obeys laws whose operation "comes before all the plans conceived by the legislator to rule or maintain them". The life of societies runs its course in the world of time; but for what part of time does the legislator promulgate his laws? It cannot be either for the past, or for the present (that line without thickness which is simply neither past nor future). It must therefore be for the future. But we are powerless to foresee the future.

The progress of the past may cast its shadow before, so that you may have a rough notion that society is to go on increasing in people, in wealth, and in knowledge, as it has increased in past time; but what shape that increase is to take, how rapid is to be the progress, and what are to be the new relations, both among individuals and among nations, it will call into existence—what new trades, what new arts may arise—what new habits, manners, customs, and opinions will be formed—what is the precise outline society will assume, with all the fillings-in of the picture to the most minute touches;—all these things, to which laws ought to be adapted, cannot possibly be known: and inquiry into them, with a view of making laws to accord with them, must necessarily make the whole business of legislation appear in its true character to mankind—a mockery of their interests, and a fraud on their understandings.[1]

[1] *Ibid.*, p. 11.

All the legislator can do is to clothe this unknowable future in the forms of the past which he does know. All legislation, therefore, is essentially of a conservative and conventional character, and can neither foresee nor desire changes in the human race. It is at this point that Godwin's criticism is taken up by Hodgskin.

Laws, considered in their origin, have, in fact, been the work of those who first obtained a monopoly of power—"man who had no profession but war and knew no trade but robbery and pillage". Their descendants still exercise this power. This had been the theory, first of Godwin, then of Paine; but Hodgskin brings it up to date and makes it precise by his examination of the origin of the existing laws of property. With the progress of mankind, he argues, the right of landed property obeys a natural law of evolution: a smaller area of land is required for each individual's existence among a pastoral than a hunting people, a smaller among an agricultural than a pastoral, and a smaller still in an industrial nation than in a nation of simple cultivators.[1] There came a time when the civilized world was invaded by barbarian hordes who had not risen above the mental level of the pastoral peoples. They brought with them ideas on the quantity of land necessary for a man's livelihood, which were out of date in comparison with those of the world which they invaded, and they appropriated the land of the conquered nations in accordance with their own ideas.[2] From this arose the opposition, still funda-

[1] *Nat. and Art. Right of Property*, pp. 63–7.
[2] *Ibid.*, pp. 69–70.

mental under different forms in all the western world, between the *natural right* and the *legal* or *artificial right* of ownership.

The persons who thus appropriated the soil of Europe, did so by a right of conquest. . . . Power so acquired, and privileges so established, were the basis of the present *political and legal*, not social, edifice of Europe. These conquerors were the first legislators . . . the power of legislation has continued in the hands of their descendants to the present day. . . . The law . . . is a set of rules and practices laid down and established, partly by the legislator, partly by custom, and partly by the judges, supported and enforced by all the power of the government, and intended as far as our subject is concerned, to secure the appropriation of the whole annual produce of labour. Nominally these rules and practices are said to have for their object to secure property in land; to appropriate tithes, and to procure a revenue for the government; actually and in fact they are intended to appropriate to the law-makers the produce of those who cultivate the soil, prepare clothing, or distribute what is produced among the different classes, and among different communities. Such is law.[1]

Government, in other words, is the instrument of economic domination for the landowners, who protect their property by laws conceived for this purpose, for the priests, who preach obedience to the laws and receive in exchange "a part of the legislation and of the annual product of labour", and, for the capitalists, who are the constant allies of the government, the Church and the landowners. The capitalists, undoubtedly, constitute a class more difficult to define than the others because they are very often also workers, but certainly, "in so much

[1] *Ibid.*, pp. 46–7, 72–3.

as they are", thay have "no natural right to the large part of the annual product that the law guarantees them". How, in these circumstances, is it possible to count on the government official and the soldier to repress the crime and theft of which, historically, they were the earliest authors? Penal laws, elaborated to defend an artificial right of ownership, are powerless to command respect for it.

> They inflict pain, but they produce no amendment, and impose no salutary control. What is generally benefical, what is commanded by Nature, needs not to be enforced by laws; what is intended for the benefit of a sect or a class and not agreeable to her commands, men seek to maintain by terror and pain.[1]

The true end of the law is "the defence of the power of the legislator". Is not that admitted by this strange philosophy which asks explicitly for the sacrifice of individuals, who alone are real, to society, to the state and to the law?[2]

Fortunately, if human laws are powerless for good, they are also powerless for evil. If there really are "laws of nature", "decrees of nature", can one say, without involving oneself in paradox, that these decrees can be violated? Actually, replies Hodgskin,

> we can trespass on physical laws, but not with impunity. Both in the material and moral world the commands of nature are only known to us through our own pleasures and pains. If we run our head against a post, she warns us by the pain that it is harder than our skull, and commands us to make use of our eyes. . . . When we examine the question of property, we shall in like manner find that much misery is caused by our opposing the natural right

[1] *Nat. and Art. Right of Property*, p. 158.
[2] *Ibid.*, pp. 45–6.

of property. Nature warns us against that by pain, in the same manner as she warns us to respect the laws of gravity.[1]

Therefore, societies prosper to the extent to which they obey the laws of nature; and, therefore, in the long run, natural laws should triumph. What is law taken by itself? A fragment of parchment. What is it that ensures its execution? Law does not exist nor is it finally established except by the tolerance of the public. Do away with law, and public opinion will be sufficient to guarantee the respect of rights.

If you will but put aside the statute-book, and the legislator and the judge, and look into society, you will see, that the greater part of the rights of men and of women, of neighbours and friends, of parents and children, of common acquaintances, and even of those who live in hostility, for they have rights, you will see that most of our domestic and civil rights, the dearest and the best, are not guaranteed by any law, and have no other security but the mutual respect of man for man, or the moral feelings of individuals.[2]

But suppose on the contrary that law, unsupported by public opinion, is the product of a legislator's arbitrary power; it is then null and void.

The individual law-maker soon runs his course, his successor has whims of his own, and cares not to employ his military power to enforce obedience to some whim of his predecessor.[3]

Opinion, however, which commands the legislator, itself obeys "physical circumstances", laws of nature. Indeed,

when we look at the great number of laws restricting industry, and at the great number intended to exact a

[1] *Ibid.*, p. 59. [2] *Ibid.*, pp. 135–6. [3] *Ibid.*, p. 116.

revenue for the government, rent for the landowner, tithes for the priests, and profit for the capitalist, we feel more surprised that industry should have survived the immense burdens laid on it, than that a few thieves should prefer living by open plunder, risking the punishment of the laws, to a life of unrewarded labour. That men yet labour at all, is an admirable contradiction of the law-makers' base assertion, I say base, because it is made for a base purpose—that men are naturally averse from labour.[1]

Writing the history of societies, therefore, Hodgskin maintains, does not mean writing the history of positive laws; for the progress of society takes place according to a natural law in spite of governments. Research should instead be undertaken into "some of the great alterations in society, of which they were the imperfect copies".[2] In spite of the law landed property has been subdivided, and the revenues of clergy and of government have diminished: the progress of capitalism has been the great fact of modern history.

The capitalist was originally a labourer, or the descendant of a villain, and he obtained profit on what he was able to save from the produce of his own labour, after he had wrested his liberty from his masters, because he was then able to make them respect his right to use the product of his own industry. But what he then received, and now receives, under the name of profit, is a portion of the wealth annually created by labour. In fact the capitalist has obtained the whole of the landlord's power, and his right to have profit is a right to receive a portion of the produce of the landlord's slaves.[3]

This progress is a natural movement to the extent to

[1] *Nat. and Art. Right of Property*, p. 54.
[2] *Ibid.*, p. 115.
[3] *Ibid.*, p. 98.

which it has been brought about, first by respect for the natural rights of property, and then by the growth in the number and the wealth of the emancipated slaves. It is a movement which has thwarted all the legislative efforts aimed at its repression and retardation. (One thinks especially of the usury laws.) Now, by a continuation of the same progress, a new age is going to succeed the age of capitalism.

Now we find, in consequence of the respect of the natural right of property, that a large middle class, completely emancipated from the bondage and destitution which the law, by fixing the rate both of wages and interest, sought to perpetuate, has grown up in every part of Europe, uniting in their own persons the character both of labourers and capitalists. They are fast increasing in numbers; and we may hope, as the beautiful inventions of art gradually supersede unskilled labour, that they, reducing the whole society to equal and free men, will gradually extinguish all that yet remains of slavery and oppression.[1]

Is it necessary to describe this future society, founded on respect for the natural rights of property? Those who believe in the efficacy of legislation and who consider progress to be the work of a system of laws—mechanical, reasoned and preconceived—think it is possible to trace a picture of it. As for me, declares Hodgskin,

though our present system is wrong, I am not bound, in order to satisfy their unholy craving to regulate what no individual does or can comprehend, viz. *society*, for it is yet in progress, or is not yet fully created, all its phenomena not being yet unfolded to our understanding; I am not bound, though present legislation be bad, to suggest

[1] *Ibid.*, p. 101.

some legislation which would be better. Society is a natural phenomenon, and I inquire into the laws which regulate it, as I would inquire into the laws which regulate the course of the seasons. To suppose that the control of them is given into our hands has been set down as madness by one of our greatest moralists. To those who having, century after century, tried in vain to regulate society and determine its course, who, foreseeing none of the great changes which have occurred in personal rights, and in the right of property, have been gradually compelled to make their legislation conform to the circumstances of society, I willingly leave the task, as they of course foresee its future condition, of projecting schemes and prescribing laws for its welfare. I only aim at ascertaining natural laws, and, seeing that with them legislation is in conflict, I reject it, trusting the welfare of society, which I do not comprehend, to the same benevolent Power which overruling, in past times, the decrees of the lawmaker, has ever established and upheld order, and has conducted mankind so far on the glorious career, which, judging from past changes, we may hope they have yet to run.[1]

[1] *Nat. and Art. Right of Property*, pp. 160–1.

CHAPTER THREE

1832 – 1869

Years of Journalism – *The Economist* – The Two Lectures of 1857

Just as Hodgskin was publishing his letters to Lord Brougham the electoral reforms of 1832 were finally accomplished. Hodgskin appreciated their importance but did not consider them as definitive. The real question underlying all others for him was that of the rights of property.

The growth of humanity, the general love of liberty, and the general hatred of oppression, prevent the existence of any odious and revolting cruelty in any part of Europe; but avarice and profusion are yet unchecked; and the contest, a very ignoble one, is simply who shall have most riches. . . . To relieve this distress, only one of two things can possibly be done; either the quantity of wealth must be augmented, or it must be better and differently distributed. . . . As those political changes have not effected, and cannot effect the expected benefits, men will necessarily turn away from political alterations as unproductive of good, and inquire into the sources of evil, and means of drying them up. They must come to that great source, the opposition between the legal and the natural right of property. . . .[1]

Far from resolving this problem, the Reform Act would perhaps only serve to aggravate its acuteness.

[1] *Nat. and Art. Right of Property*, pp. 14, 170, 172–3.

For experience proved, he contended, that every change of government worsened the economic situation of nations, provoked crises, increased burdens and was a cause of misery and disappointment.[1]

This discontent had brought Hodgskin disciples. "Those who were disappointed in Mr. Owen's promises and prediction [fell] as it were into the snare of Mr. Thomas Hodgskin, who by his lecturing and publishing induced thousands to believe that every thing produced belonged to the individual producers each in his own right."[2] At the Mechanics' Institute in London where a "numerous and attentive audience"[3] listened to his lectures, he had become an influential adviser of Dr. Birkbeck and, to the great anger of James Mill[4] and the Benthamites, he had attained a position of similar influence over Black, the publisher of the *Morning Chronicle*, of whose political views he was the inspirer. The defenders of capitalism were aroused to refute him. One such was Samuel Read in his *Natural Grounds of Right to Vendible Property* of 1829.[5] Some members of Robert Owen's co-operatives had no doubt read his *Labour Defended* in America, and in 1830 Thomas Cooper, the American economist, in the second edition of his *Lessons in Political Economy*, took this book as a text in his refutation of the new

[1] *Nat. and Art. Right of Property*, pp. 171–2.

[2] B.M. Add. MSS., 27, 791, f. 263.

[3] *Pop. Pol. Ec.*, p. viii.

[4] Mill to Brougham, 3 September 1832; Bain, *Life of James Mill*, p. 364.

[5] *Natural Grounds of Right to Vendible Property*, 1829, pp. xxi and 127–8. Hodgskin has undoubtedly misspelt the name of the author at *Nat. and Art. Right of Property*, p. 171.

tendencies of what he called the "mechanic Political Economists".[1] In 1831 Charles Knight, whose violence exasperated Hodgskin, warned the lower classes, to whom he addressed his works of popularisation, against the dangers of the new teaching. "Such doctrines may begin in the lecture-room, and there look harmless as abstract propositions; but they end in the maddening passion, the drunken frenzy, the unappeasable tumult—the plunder, the fire, and the blood."[2]

Hodgskin, stimulated by this success and by this very opposition, might have continued his research in political economy and become the theorist of the nascent English socialist movement; but his investigations into the production and distribution of wealth were, as he said in 1832, only an "episode of a much greater work on criminal law".

> Legislators are yet completely ignorant of the first elements of criminal legislation, and the correct and philosophic answer to the meaning question, "What is crime?" throws down at one blow the whole theoretical structure of penal enactments. By a deduction from principles not here enunciated, the author has satisfied himself that all law-making, except gradually and quietly to repeal all existing laws, is arrant humbug.[3]

Would he, then, complete this great work on the ideas of law and punishment which he had been contemplating for so many years? In the event,

[1] *Lectures*, 2nd edn., 1830, Chap. XXXI and, in particular, pp. 349, 351, 352.

[2] *The Rights of Industry*, addressed to the working men of the United Kingdom, by the author of *The Results of Machinery*. II. Capital and Labour, pp. 152–3. See also pp. 56, 57, 58, 208.

[3] *Nat. and Art. Right of Property*, p. 1.

Hodgskin, now the father of seven children and compelled to work to provide for this entire family, disappeared after 1832 into the obscurity of anonymous journalism. He wrote, not only for the *Morning Chronicle*, but for the *Daily News*, the *Courier* and later the *Sun*; for many years until his death he sent a weekly article to the *Brighton Guardian*; he was one of the editors of the *Illustrated London News*; he collaborated for a long time with Thomas Hansard in the publication of the *Parliamentary Reports*.[1] In spite of his absorption in these tasks, he took part, as a popular lecturer, in the Chartist agitation to establish universal suffrage. But, no doubt because of the violence of the Chartists and of their appeals for the state to intervene with legislation in social questions, he became disgusted with revolutionary and socialist radicalism and was brought round with others to the party of Cobden and the agitation for Free Trade. At this time, in 1846, he came to *The Economist*, newly established by Wilson: once again, if not through books, at least by considered articles, he would be able to take up the work of the theoretician and social philosopher.

Given the responsibility for analysing new works on social science and political economy, he continued to affirm that political economy, with its rigorous proofs and optimistic conclusions, is alone

[1] Hodgskin was also editor of the short-lived *London Telegraph*, a midday newspaper launched by Herbert Ingram in 1848. On the newspaper's failure, Ingram found a scapegoat in his editor, who, he said, had used the word "bureaucracy" at least ten times in one week in leading articles. See H. R. Fox Bourne, *English Newspapers* (1887), II, 235.—*Translator.*

among the supposed sciences of mankind in meriting the name of science.

. . . all other matters connected with politics being but tradition, ground work, assumption, fancy, usurpation or expediency, there is no other science in politics but political economy.[1]

Political, or rather *social* economy: for him the first epithet makes nonsense when the question is that of giving a name to a science which essentially postulates the non-intervention of politicians in social affairs.[2] "That there neither exists nor can exist a political science was the theme developed by Hodgskin in the study which he devoted in 1852[3] to Cornewall Lewis' treatise *On the Methods of Reasoning and Observation in Politics.* Politics, he maintains, is a constantly changing discipline of which it can only be said that it runs a parallel course of progress to that of society, a progress whose history can be told but about which no theory can be formulated.

Government is obviously analogous to all the arts which men commence instinctively and empirically, which subsequently lead to the science of agriculture, navigation, metallurgy, etc.; but these sciences relate rather to the properties of soils and the laws of vegetable life, to the conformation of the earth and some motions of the heavenly bodies by which ships are guided over the ocean, and to the properties of the rude practices that have ever prevailed in tilling the ground, in sailing or rowing from place to place, or in melting and forging metals. Besides the practices of man through ages in these arts, of which

[1] *The Economist*, 7 April 1855, pp. 370–1.
[2] *Ibid.*, 12 December 1846, pp. 1621–2.
[3] *Ibid.*, November 1852, pp. 1326–7.

there is not a science distinct from their history, there are in all these cases, and in all cases in which arts give birth to science, a subject matter distinct from man himself. In politics there is only one, man, his arts, and his practices, and of them exclusively, as distinct from the science of human nature, there can be no separate science. There is science of the production and distribution of wealth, but that, like the science of navigation and agriculture, concerns material objects distinct from man; and, although it intimately concerns all his arts, his motives, his existence, still the science is not limited exclusively to those arts, or to his practices and existence, but has a visible and tangible subject-matter in which labour is incorporated and become wealth, distinct from man himself.

Moreover—and perhaps above all—can it be affirmed, without self-contradiction, that political science implies both the idea of nationality and the idea that the progress of the human race tends to efface differences of nationality? Politics will lose its peculiar object, he asserts, in proportion to the progress of civilisation.

Politics is wholly founded, as Mr. Lewis says, on nationality. Its essence is that each sovereign people should have a government of its own.

But

the progress of society, not political progress, has been, since the beginning of history, continually to expand the bounds of nationality—to incorporate tribes into communities, communities into nations, till one nation has attracted many. There has been, therefore, a gradual, natural and necessary annihilation of that peculiar circumstance or principle on which all politics are founded. . . . Human nature may have been identical at different epochs, though this is doubted; but the basis of politics is evanescent. There can be no science except of what is permanent; and nationality not being permanent like the planets, there can be no political science.

It may be true, as Mr. Lewis says, that the *science* of political economy refers to the relation of men living in political society, and cannot but refer to them since men from the beginning of history have always lived in political society. Yet it may at the same time be true that the principles of the science of the product of wealth may altogether be contrary, as we know they are in many cases, to the practice of political society, and, far from being subservient to it, may be destined to subvert it.

The historian, therefore, ought not to explain social progress as the result of the accidental and haphazard interventions of legislators and wise men. Only the "presumption of the educated classes" could attribute the progress of modern Europe to the influence of thinkers and philosophers.[1]

By no direct help from any mental or other science, since Locke's time the *mind* or society has escaped from a multitude of prejudices, and has expanded in every direction. With and by time the *mind* enlarges or expands. Scientific discoveries and the arts built on them are neither made fortuitously nor by man's design; they are a regular and progressive development which no conduct of the human understanding—though care in this respect may make individuals good, knowing and wise—could ever bring about.[2]

Hodgskin did not want the government to take upon itself the task of directing and accelerating progress by a system of state education. In 1847 and 1848 he led a campaign against the Education

[1] *The Economist*, 21 October 1848, pp. 1190–1201.
[2] *Ibid.*, 16 September 1854, p. 1021.

Bill, which Macaulay was supporting,[1] and attacked Macaulay on the basis of the latter's own philosophy of history. Has not Macaulay affirmed, he declares, that the great English revolutions could not have been produced "by legislative enactment or the use of physical force"? Macaulay is wrong only in considering the general underlying forces in history to be of a moral and religious character. If England has been more quickly civilised and emancipated than the nations of the Continent, it is simply because the population, confined within the limits of an island, has at an early stage became denser than in the rest of Europe. In short, for Hodgskin, among historical factors, the one whose influence predominates is not the political or the legal, nor the moral or religious, but the economic. Hodgskin's philosophy of history, what he calls "the history of civilisation" or "the natural history of man considered as a progressive animal", is, in the correct sense of the word, an historical materialism, excellently defined by him when he congratulates Thiers for having clearly observed

> that the fact of property existed in the beginning of society, before the idea of property was formed, or, in other words, the fact that property is a right preceded the opinion that it ought to be guaranteed and preserved. It may therefore be assumed that actual changes in property would in all subsequent times precede all the political opinions and changes connected with them. Such an assumption is consistent with the general fact that all man's knowledge, political and other knowledge, and

[1] *The Economist*, 20 March 1847, pp. 323–4; 24 April 1847, pp. 462–4; 1 May 1847, pp. 492–4; 30 December 1848, pp. 1471–3.

ultimately all man's opinions are corrected by, and therefore modelled on, the facts of the material world. Mind when most enlightened and informed is a correct reflection of external nature. In the long run, therefore, that, according to the laws on which man must act to live, will shape and govern all his opinions.[1]

But if Hodgskin considered political economy as the true science of society, furnishing the key to the philosophy of history, he remained the determined opponent of Ricardo's system. When in 1846 MacCulloch published the complete edition of his master's works, Hodgskin regretted that MacCulloch had fulfilled his duty as editor badly in so far as he had not tried to determine impartially

how much of his reputation was merely ephemeral, the result of extrinsic circumstances, and how much of it is the lasting consequence of the important truths he discovered and embodied in his great work.

And Hodgskin, taking up the function of criticism neglected by MacCulloch, blames Ricardo for having obtained, through his incontestable competence in banking and finance, a reputation as an economist which he did not deserve, and for having observed economic phenomena between 1815 and 1820 in a period of crisis, in which such phenomena presented an abnormal appearance. Once again Hodgskin brings all his own criticisms to bear on Ricardo.[2]

Ricardo, he argues, obscured when he claimed to clarify the theory of value as defined by Adam Smith.

[1] *Ibid.*, 30 December 1848, pp. 1480–1.
[2] *Ibid.*, 28 November 1846, pp. 1556–8.

In one sense, Smith's verbal variation from his own principle serves better to explain some social phenomena than Mr. Ricardo's technical adherence to it. Clearly the increase of *price* which Smith indicated to be caused by rent and profit meant the increase of labour, which the labourer, who originally possessed the whole commodity produced, had to give, for the same, or an equal commodity, when he, not other men, not certainly the capitalists and the landlords, had to pay profit and rent, or share that commodity with others. Substituting labourer for labour, in Smith's doctrine, it is a truer representation of what actually occurs in society than Mr. Ricardo's, which, after all, is of comparatively little importance, because it is limited entirely to the exchangeable *variations in the value of commodities*, and takes no notice of the exchange between the different classes of labourers, capitalists, and landowners, which it was partly Smith's object to explain. Admitting the greater verbal or logical accuracy of Mr. Ricardo, it was obtained, we apprehend, by shutting entirely out of his science those important relations of the labourer to other classes, which Smith, by a change in his terms, really discussed.

In relation to wages, Ricardo admits that different kinds of labour are differently valued; then he proceeds to envisage nothing but quantitative variations of labour; and yet

the comparative degree of estimation in which different kinds of human labour are held is precisely the thing of which a peasant complains when he says that he gets only 7s. a week, whilst a Minister of State, a Field Marshal, an Archbishop, or an overseer of other labourers, gets as many or three times as many pounds a day. . . . We say nothing about the rectitude of any rate of payment, but he must be blind to what is going on in society who is insensible to the facts that *inequalities* of *reward*, or comparative degrees of estimation in which different kinds of human labour are held, and consequently different rates of wages, is one of the agitating topics of the day; and the work which, pretending to treat of the greatest of the social sciences, expressly excludes the subject from consideration, casts out a topic, which Adam Smith discussed, of almost overwhelming interest.

Hodgskin took up without modification his old theory of capital. In 1854 he upheld it against Morrison, the author of an *Essay on the relations of capital and labour*,[1] Rickards, the author of a book on *Population and Capital*,[2] and Charles Knight, who had just amended and published under a new title the work in which, in 1832, he had dealt so harshly with Hodgskin.[3]

It is contradictory to say that *capital* is the result of labour, and that capital must precede all production. . . . "Industry", says Mr. Rickards, "is limited by capital." In what sense? Not as to its value nor as to its quantity, for the former depends on the skill of the labourers, and the latter on their energy. The savings of a Russian nobleman and an English manufacturer may be equally 10,000 quarters of wheat, and the industry fed by each of the 10,000 quarters will be obviously very different in value and in quantity. . . . Employment, or the turning of capital quickly, depends in this case on a sentiment: the fund is rather one man crediting another, or believing that there will be future production to pay him for present exertions than goods now in existence; but certainly without one atom more or less of capital, as confidence and credit exist or not, the working classes may be well employed and well paid, or doomed to idleness and starvation. If Mr. Morrison had studied man and his motives

[1] *The Economist*, 29 April 1854, pp. 458–9.

[2] *Ibid.*, 18 November 1854, pp. 1269–70.

[3] *Ibid.*, 30 December 1854, pp. 1453–4. See further a letter addressed to the *Morning Chronicle*, 23 January 1858, under the heading *Trade without capital.*

more—the immaterial relations of human beings rather than the relations of material things—his book would have been more profound. . . . Man is the sole productive agent. . . . The whole science of political economy concerns man and industry, not his products.

Finally, asserts Hodgskin, the theory of differential rent is outmoded. He congratulates Carey[1] for having, in criticising it, added one more attempt to

the numerous attempts now making in various parts of the world, and in various directions, to show that the government of society is provided for by higher laws than those of human legislation . . . to establish the authority of nature.

Doubtless the arguments of Carey do not always apply. To show that a man cultivates the light soil before he cultivates the heavy is not to show that he begins by cultivating the less fertile soil. Light soils are, in the first place, from the strictly economic standpoint adopted by Ricardo, the most fertile soils. But Carey, for Hodgskin, has the merit of setting facts drawn from the economic history of the United States against the very small number of facts which had struck Ricardo's imagination, an imagination "more penetrating than informed". At a time when there was a very rapid growth of population on a limited area of land,

from the then rapid increase of rent Mr. Ricardo inferred its origin, and ascribed that to different degrees of fertility in the soil, and to the occupation first of the most fertile land which history shows was the result of conquest and oppression.

[1] *The Economist*, 28 October 1848, pp. 1227–8.

Fundamentally, asks Hodgskin, was not Ricardo's pessimism surprising in an age when the productive energies of the civilised world were undergoing a prodigious development?

The important conclusion, that in the progress of society land yields a less and less return to capital and labour . . . is a contradiction of Mr. Ricardo's own principle, and the main principle of the science—that labour pays all cost. He did something to clear that from doubts and anomalies, and since his time it has been continually and generally admitted that labour is the sole source of value, the sole source of production, the payment of all cost, and the ultimate regulator of price. Land may be left entirely out of view, but labour, as it becomes enlightened by knowledge, giving birth in the progress of society to exquisite skill, whether employed in draining or cultivating the ground, constructing and using the machinery of manufacture, is notoriously more and more productive. Mr. Ricardo adverts continually to improvements in cultivation and to discoveries in art as tending at intervals to check the gravitation of profits, but that which he speaks of as exceptions to the rule, are in fact the rule, and constitute the great law of population and production. Man becomes skilful as the species becomes more numerous.

Moreover, is not the theory of differential rent so outmoded thirty years after its discovery that it is not worth the trouble of discussion?

Though there may be no accredited refutation of them extant in words, society has practically lived them down, and nobody, except a few mere writers, now troubles himself about Malthus on Population or Ricardo on Rent.[1]

The very decadence of Ricardian orthodoxy, indeed, seemed calculated to give confidence to

[1] *Ibid.*, 18 November 1854, p. 1269.

Hodgskin in his own theories. John Stuart Mill, in his great work, had just made a distinction, rather as Hodgskin himself had done, between natural laws and human laws, particularly those human laws which claim to define the rights of property and thereby influence economic phenomena.[1] Mill, according to Hodgskin, has perhaps only lacked a sense of history and his book would have more value,

> if the long dissertations on tenure of land were distinctly shown to refer to particular conditions of society which tolerate and justify at one time, as to land, what is intolerable and monstrously injust and injurious to another. The original appropriation of soil, for example, many centuries ago, was then a bearable evil; but its influence on the present condition of society particularly in Ireland, has obviously become nothing less than destructive.

And he finds himself equally obliged to regret that Mill, probably a slave to those legislative prejudices dear to the Benthamite school, has, after admitting the existence of natural laws of production, held the distribution of wealth to be absolutely arbitrary and dependent on the legislator and the customs which he might chance to establish.

> Men may do wrong but cannot escape the consequences; from which it follows that there is a right and wrong in the distribution of wealth, as well as in the protecting or taking life; and that a nation can no more decree what distribution of wealth it likes, or protect the distribution it decrees by force, than it can neglect to till its fields, or than it can ravage another nation's territories, and commit all kinds of atrocities, without violating the moral laws.

[1] *The Economist*, 27 May 1848, pp. 603–4.

If the supposedly natural laws of the distribution of wealth formulated by the Ricardians have to be refuted, it is precisely because, tending to impute to nature economic evil and, as a result, every kind of social evil, they deny the true law of natural justice.

Is this to say that Hodgskin's thought had shown no change since 1832? It had, in fact, undergone undeniable changes, but their importance will be differently appreciated according to the standpoint from which his philosophy is interpreted. Hodgskin continued[1] to affirm that the right of property, "as it is legally constituted, is not capable of improvement", and that "the distribution of wealth is the social problem of the day", but he did not desire "a great alteration in property, so much the more [*sic*] a communist or socialist system, to suppress its present distribution". If Hodgskin is thought of as one of the first to furnish English socialists with an economic doctrine, the change will be found to be serious; but it will seem less so, if it is remembered that Hodgskin always fought, on principle, against every intervention of the government and the law in the distribution of wealth, and that he criticised the revenues of the landowner and the capitalist precisely because he attributed a legislative and governmental origin to them.

Hodgskin found the existing constitution of the rights of property unjust and injurious in its effects. But, except by violating the individualistic and anarchist principle of his social philosophy, he could never have asked government to intervene, either to

[1] *Ibid.*, 26 May 1849, p. 584.

institute collective ownership of the soil or to reduce ownership to its natural dimensions by force. In 1851 there appeared Herbert Spencer's *Social Statistics* and Hodgskin welcomed with enthusiasm a book[1] which, he wrote, "is distinguished by good feeling and will mark an epoch in the literature of scientific morality". Indeed, when, in relation to the definition of natural law—and in contrast to the Benthamite theory of law—very striking similarities are to be found between Spencer's book and the open letters addressed by Hodgskin to Lord Brougham in 1832, when, moreover, it is noted that Spencer worked on *The Economist* for several successive years and was in daily contact with Hodgskin, visiting his home, asking his advice and borrowing books from his library, is not there justification for believing it possible that Hodgskin exercised a direct influence on Spencer? But Spencer inclined towards a kind of agrarian communism and on this point Hodgskin was at variance with him. This type of communism, he declares, involves the confusion of the right of the individual to the use of his faculties with his right to the use of the soil: it does not take account of the fact that, with the progress of the arts, an increasing number of individuals can work and receive the product of their labour without sharing in the possession of the soil; it withdraws from individuals the right of ownership to give that right to society, when "societies have no other rights than the sum of the rights of individuals"; it is forgetful of the fact that rights exist only by the consent of opinion, and that, in consequence, if

[1] *The Economist*, 8 February 1851, pp. 149–51.

opinion agrees to the appropriation of the soil by the individual, it is because it believes it sees in it a social good. Finally,

> his plan of giving the land to the public, and making those who cultivate it pay for its use, would be in fact to take away from the cultivators a part of the produce of their labour—for it is an error to suppose the land produces anything—and would be to bestow that on other men, alias the public. It would be a violation of property, and a terrible check to industry. Some attachment, perhaps, to yet lingering prejudices derived from landlordism, may lead the writer in this instance into error. He adopts, we believe unconsciously, the notion that the rent now paid for land is the representation of, and is equivalent to, the capital invested in the land by successive generations, combined with an unjust conquest of its original owners. All the land of England has been bought over and over again. Land, we repeat produces nothing to satisfy human wants more than the ocean and the air. In general it must be cleared before it can be used. What is usually called the produce of land is the produce of labour applied to the land; and to take away the produce of individual labour applied to the land, or any part of it, and give it to the public, is a violation of the right of property in labour and in its products.

Twenty years earlier Hodgskin would not have taxed as "prejudiced" the view that rent expresses an ancient legal right, the right of force and conquest. But one phrase, written off-handedly, cannot be held to prevent this development, taken as a whole, from conforming with the principles of his economic philosophy. If labour alone, to the exclusion of the natural qualities of the soil, is truly the real cause and the measure of value, the state no more than the landowner should be able to appropriate a part of the produce of the cultivator's labour. Hodgskin did not set himself apart from the ordinary radicals, from Cobden and Bright, when, in the matter of landed wealth, he confined himself to advocating the suppression of outdated laws and the emancipation of the soil whose sale was impeded by a multitude of laws, when he applauded the Irish Encumbered Estates Act[1] and demanded, in a century of universal free trade, the establishment of free trade in land.[2] But he remained faithful to his principles when he limited the obligations of the legislator to this negative task: for it had been shown, and by Hodgskin himself,

> that the portions in which it [land] should be divided amongst them [individuals] . . . is nothing the state can settle beforehand, because it depends at every moment on the amount of population in a given space, and on their knowledge and skill, of which the state or any union of men must be ignorant till it has come into existence.[3]

There remain the profits of capitalism: does it not seem that Hodgskin, in growing older, had become more indulgent to them? In 1825[4] he took his stand, in his criticism of capital, on the law, enunciated by Ricardo, of the inverse variation of profits and wages. Now one of his grounds of attack on Ricardo was that

> he puts the wages of the labourer and the profits of the capitalist in opposition, and regards the one as a deduction from the other. These are fatal errors. We are not fully

[1] *Our chief crime: cause and cure*, 1857, pp. 11–13.

[2] *The Economist*, 13 December 1856, p. 1371.

[3] *Ibid.*, 20 January 1849, pp. 72–3.

[4] [The 1815 of the original would again appear to be a misprint. —*Translator*.]

satisfied . . . that capitalists and labourers may both get more and become better provided for by means of an improvement in productive power. . . .[1]

In 1825 he counted on workers' combinations to protect the interests of the wage-earners against the demands of the capitalists. Now he condemned in its entirety

the interferences between capital and labour by Communists, Socialists, and combinations (they are all evil). . . . The principles of observing the natural law and not interfering with them is as imperative on Governments as on Communists, Socialists, and combining workmen. In fact, the interference of the former is the parent of the interference of the latter.[2]

But if these expressions reveal an evolution in his thinking, do they not even more reveal the radical infirmity of his doctrine? It is the desire of justice and nature, according to Hodgskin, that every individual shall receive the whole produce of his labour. But will every individual be obliged to consume all the produce? Or will he prefer to exploit for himself the fixed capital, which his work has produced over and above the quantity of the product which he requires for his own consumption? Or again, will he be free to advance this capital to other workers? (Hodgskin appears to admit the legitimacy of these advances.) And in this last instance, can it be conceded that a system of perfect freedom will suffice in the long run to ensure to each of the contracting parties, the producer and the exploiter of capital, that part of the wage which is

[1] *The Economist*, 28 November 1846, p. 1558.
[2] *Ibid.*, 26 April 1854, pp. 458–9.

his due? But the producer of the original fixed capital is not immortal: when he has gone, who is to benefit by his savings and inventions? The state? Hodgskin's philosophy precludes him from contemplating this possibility. The exploiters of his capital and processes? In that case the state would have to intervene to restrict the freedom, which the producer might claim, of transmitting his wealth by gift, inheritance or will. But if this power to restrict is accepted, the legitimacy of this transmission and, at the same time, the legitimacy of capitalist accumulation have to be admitted. Hodgskin, not wanting new laws against usury, confines himself to the hope that

> the gradual progress of society, by which capital and labour seem more and more to become united in the same hands is perhaps the more appropriate, just, and easy solution of the difficulty.

He relies on the multiplication of joint-stock companies, on the association of employers and workmen, and in this puts himself singularly close to the ordinary radicals.[1] This was because since 1832 the English socialists had become either so many revolutionaries, thinking to prepare the reign of justice by a sudden and violent revolution and not by a gradual evolution, or so many interventionists demanding, with the support of certain Tories, new laws and regulations to protect them against the employers. The public, says Hodgskin, is beginning again to consider with favour

> the false notion that one or two leading minds—a Louis Blanc, a M. Lamartine, a Lord Ashley—can model

[1] *The Economist*, 17 March 1849, pp. 303–4.

society, and that society cannot be helped but by some such forming mind. . . .[1]

And the names chosen as examples (two revolutionaries and a Socialist Tory) are characteristic. If a choice has to be made between bourgeois free-trade and working-class "interventionism", Hodgskin is unable to accept the second which seems to him to be a contradiction in terms. He sees in free trade, not a universal panacea, but the first step in a process which will end by curing all social ills. In 1854 he discovered that pauperism was growing. He explained this in these terms:

. . . all the general causes, whatever they may be, of pauperism are still in existence and we must not expect an approach to its total extinction till they are removed. Free trade and the gold discoveries, cheap food and a rapid increase of employment, had most beneficial effect in reducing pauperism, but their influence is no longer equal to the baneful influence which causes pauperism at all times. . . . To investigate the causes of general pauperism in society would lead us, however, far and wide; and we can only say, whatever they may be, that Free Trade was only calculated to overcome their influence for a time, and that to get rid of pauperism altogether we require a succession of Free-Trade measures, or measures removing the obstacles which ignorance and presumption have heretofore placed in the way of individual independence and social progress.[2]

In 1855 Hodgskin stopped writing his critical notices for *The Economist*. Had his views on the theory of political economy, eccentric as they still were, finally upset Wilson, the editor of the review?

[1] *Ibid.*, 21 October 1848, pp. 1190–1.
[2] *Ibid.*, 18 February 1854, p. 170.

Possibly: but as yet there was no breach between them, and Hodgskin, from November 1855 to April 1857 in a series of articles, carried out a long-standing campaign for the reform of the penal laws. This was always, in his eyes, the central problem: on it his thinking had never been troubled by the slightest doubt. The multiplicity of crimes, he states, is striking, and there is reason to believe that their number is increasing. The reactionaries, timid by nature, fix the responsibility for this presumed growth of crime upon the new industrial and commercial civilisation. Speculation is denounced, but

> without speculation we should have no railroads, no docks, no great companies. . . . Some of the most useful, greatest and richest men of the day—the Stephensons, the Petos, the Brasseys, the Barings, the Thorntons, the Rothschilds—are speculators.[1]

The desire for wealth is denounced but,

> duly analysed, it is found to be little or nothing more than the desire for the respect of one another. Beyond that, wealth only gives "meat, clothes, and fire". The honest desire is to receive services and honours for services and honours rendered. It is an integral and necessary part of society, and without it men could not live in communion.[2]

Likewise commerce is denounced but

> We are all merchants . . . and . . . trade is only mutual service by mutual dealing.[3]

Competition also is denounced but

[1] *The Economist*, 1 March 1856, p. 223.
[2] *Our chief crime*, 1857, p. 2.
[3] *Ibid.*, p. 2. *The Economist*, 1 March 1856, p. 223.

competition . . . is the soul of excellence, and gives to every man his fair reward.[1]

And finally civilisation itself is denounced

but the characteristics of savages whether discovered in modern times, or known in antiquity, are utter selfishness, and disregard of humanity, with more astuteness than honesty.[2]

Blame is laid on the factory system and the large towns: Lord Grey sees in the increase of crime "the natural consequence of a growing density of population and wealth". But

that population should increase in density, is the natural and necessary consequence of the strongest instincts of our species; that it has hitherto increased, is a certain fact: that it is destined to increase hereafter, seems as certain as that the sun should continue to rise: that all men strive to get wealth, is equally certain: and if, therefore, as the Noble Earl stated, and as the multitude have believed, that from population and wealth flow an increase of criminality, there can be no rational hope that any system of penal laws or reformatories can check the flood.[3]

After so many confused pronouncements the philosophy of the penal law remains to be formulated.

Hodgskin attempted this task; or, more precisely he verified, by thorough statistical investigations, those prejudices which for so long he had held in these matters. From the beginning of his collaboration with *The Economist* he had had the responsibility for articles about moral statistics, on the number of marriages and births, on the number of assisted

[1] *Our chief crime*, p. 3. [2] *Ibid.*, p. 3.
[3] *The Economist*, 12 January 1856, pp. 31–2.

paupers, and on the number of crimes committed and of condemnations pronounced. He was aware of the difficulties of these investigations. Social phenomena, he says, are complex and causes continue to live on in their effects long after they themselves have ceased to exist. The number of crimes ought not to be judged by the number of convictions: it can happen that a very criminal nation, because of its moral insensibility, may be very lenient in the repression of crime.[1] Besides, official statistics are badly compiled and destitute of scientific character. Hodgskin, however, believed that by a thorough and prolonged analysis of the statistics, he could establish that the cause of crime is poverty, the maldistribution of wealth, that poverty itself is the result of the violation of natural laws by human legislation, and that, for the combating of crime, reliance should not be placed on penal legislation, which is the indirect consequence of economic legislation and, what is more, the direct consequence of penal legislation itself.

Crime, he asserts, is said to have increased. But the better compiled criminal statistics bring to light the fact that all types of crimes have not shown the increase of which there is complaint. The number of crimes against the person has remained stationary, if it has not been effectively lessened; it is crime against property which has become more frequent. Again, the statistics cannot furnish exact information on the increase of this second type of offence: how far is it possible to say, in relation to the number of crimes actually committed against the person,

[1] *The Economist*, 22 September 1849, pp. 1058–61.

how many are due to the instinct of revenge and how many to the spirit of gain and the desire for enrichment? Is it the case, then, that penal legislation has been more skilful in overtaking crimes against the person than in overtaking those against property? In no wise; but that is because, among the rights of the individual, the right to life is more easy to define than the rights of property. Being more comprehensible it is sooner respected and guaranteed by public opinion, without legislative or governmental control. For the rights of property are complex and changing; they are social rights and,

> as the individual is not born mature, but grows, and has different rights, and different duties, as boy or man, girl or woman, so society is not created mature, but grows as population multiplies, and as it grows, it modifies *social* rights.[1]

Legislators and governors, in claiming to fix, to immobilise, what, by its nature, changes unceasingly, are responsible in part for the increase in the number of crimes against property.

Moreover, the lesson of statistics is that the growth in the number of crimes against property has not been uniform and constant since the beginning of the century. Hodgskin, with the support of figures, makes it clear that variations in the amount of crime have followed variations in public wealth. There exists, he declares,

> a close and intimate connexion between poverty and crime, between want of prosperity and numerous offences, between want of food and vast social disorder. . . . Con-

[1] *Our chief crime*, p. 5; cf. *The Economist*, 1 March and 8 March 1856, pp. 223–53.

nexion between poverty and crime . . . [is] like substance and shadow—like sound and echo. Given the degree of prosperity of trade—the amount of honestly earned comfort among a population—and past experience would enable us to state, with an almost arithmetical exactness, the rate of crime prevalent at the time.[1]

The cause of crime is not the desire for wealth but the frustration of the legitimate satisfaction of that desire as a result of the wealth's bad distribution. The number of crimes has declined each time—around 1825 and 1843—that the application of free trade policies has produced, in spite of Gladstone's famous phrase about the dangers of the concentration of capital, a more equal distribution of fortunes.[2] It may even have been the case that, in these years of decline in crime, the number of crimes of violence has remained stationary. But that does not weaken Hodgskin's thesis; for

it was not expected to lessen anger, shame, jealousy, revenge, or any emotions of that kind—it did not interfere with any criminal laws; but it did profess to lessen property, and consequently the temptation to assail property, and accordingly the number of offences against property has diminished.[3]

Corresponding to this increase in public wealth, produced by the emancipation of the nation's industry, there has been, moreover, an increase in population,

testimony . . . to the important principle . . . that the moral principle is developed as the species multiply. . . .

[1] *The Economist*, 18 May 1844, p. 811; 12 October 1844, pp. 1299–1300.

[2] *Ibid.*, 15 March 1856, pp. 280–1; 22 March 1856, pp. 306–308; 14 June 1856, pp. 645–6; 26 July 1856, pp. 813–14.

[3] *Ibid.*, 14 May 1853, p. 534.

It is full of bright hopes for the future, leading us to suppose that the golden age of our ancestors was only a prophetic ideality which our descendants are to realise.[1]

In short, argues Hodgskin, to suppress crime, all that is necessary is to suppress poverty: and to suppress poverty it is sufficient to leave it to do away with itself spontaneously, once the laws which claim to protect industry and commerce have been repealed. In this, by implication, are condemned all the legal processes on which reliance is placed to anticipate this gradual and necessary elimination of crime. For all the reasons which can be validly advanced against the efficacy of economic laws are *a fortiori* valid against the efficacy of all laws.

In almost every case of commercial regulations—for instance, the corn laws, the whole tariff, the celebrated Act of 1844, one of the latest results of the calm deliberations of Parliament under the guidance of the safest statesman of the age,—the Parliament has not been successful. These, however, all concern material and measurable objects, food, gold, money, clothing, numbers of the population, etc.; they were all modern laws, when the subjects to which they relate had been much inquired into and were supposed to be very fully known. If the wisest amongst us now make such mistakes as to these measurable objects, may it not be supposed that laws and regulations enacted long ago, when the present condition of society was never dreamed of, are not the best means for now and hereafter promoting morality and the general welfare?[2]

Hodgskin, therefore, once more takes up his criticism of the idea of law. Laws, he contends, are

[1] *Ibid.*, 20 July 1850, pp. 786–7.
[2] *Ibid.*, 17 November 1855, pp. 1260–1.

always costly in their application; they produce poverty and poverty is the cause of crime;[1] they are static in a society which is changing every moment; they are rigid but are applied to an infinitely varying substance.[2] But, above all, by their very existence, they maintain in the mind a confusion between what nature forbids and what the law condemns, between the immoral and the illegal, between natural and positive law.

> Our notions of crime and punishment . . . are hurrying the leaders of society—who aspire to direct its corporate action as contradistinguished from the separate actions of individuals, from which result all its wealth—into extraordinary contradictions. It is first assumed that crime is what is forbidden; and without much inquiry why it is forbidden, or what particular species of actions are forbidden, it is from impulse concluded that the actions which offend those who act for the corporate society are crimes; and here, instead of enforcing only nature's prohibitions, an immense number of actions—for example selling and drinking a glass of ale at a particular hour, when a man is heated and thirsty—are classed as crimes and punished.[3]

In this is to be found the explanation of the patent immorality of lawyers. Having as their trade the defence of the law because it is old and because it is the law, their moral sense always lags behind that of the rest of men and, in particular, behind that of merchants, who create, progressively and insensibly,

[1] *The Economist*, 7 June 1856, pp. 616–17.
[2] *Ibid.*, 30 March 1850, pp. 339–40.
[3] *Ibid.*, 30 September 1854, pp. 1065–6. Cf. 27 March 1852, pp. 337–8.

the spontaneous morality of natural society.[1] It is the rich who make the law.

Our penal jurisprudence, so far as property is concerned, is a species of class legislation.[2]

Its creators are those who held power before the appearance of commercial wealth, the landed proprietors and slave-owners.

On this point, as on all others, men necessarily began to act before they had acquired, or could acquire, any knowledge of the consequences of their actions. In all the States of antiquity and the middle ages, slavery prevailed in Europe, and the principles of our penal legislation were adopted in and adapted to such a condition of society. Originally they were naturally and necessarily the repressions of the arrogant will of masters. . . . Hence . . . mere brute force—the strength of a Hercules or a Samson—of all qualities was the one most admired and honoured. . . . Then it was natural that he (man) should regard this commanding quality as the means of obtaining success on all points, and he sought moral ends by similar physical means. Brute force was embodied into laws, and success was expected in the moral as in the physical world from the use of violence. . . . In spite of much experience to the contrary, especially in domestic life, the experience of schools and colleges, and ships and armies and factories, which has, at every stage, tended to convince us that the use of violence is the worst means possible of obtaining a moral end, we still venerate the principle of violence as the basis of our present code, and look for safety, virtue, and reform from the violence it ordains in the form of penalties, imprisonment, transportation, hanging and shooting. . . . The principle of violence, the hope of effecting moral improvement by the use of physical force,

[1] *Ibid.*, 23 June 1855, pp. 671–3. Cf. 15 September and 3 November 1855, pp. 1011, 1204–5.

[2] *Ibid.*, 6 September 1856, p. 982.

was at the bottom of all the religious persecutions Lord John Russell has so justly stigmatised. The same principle is still the basis of all our penal legislation.[1]

But, following the triumph of the principle of tolerance in religious matters, it is natural and necessary that the ruin of the principle of violence should one day be consummated by the disappearance of every kind of penal legislation.

Hodgskin demonstrates in detail the foolishness of the different penalties devised for the prevention of crime. If capital punishment is efficacious that is not the end sought by the legislator in instituting it. Taking up a theory already formulated on an earlier occasion in his *Travels in Germany*, he distinguishes two elements in the law: on the one hand, the solemn declaration of what nature forbids or is supposed to forbid, and, on the other, the threat of a punishment inflicted by the agents of the government, a threat designed to intimidate those who experience a real temptation to commit the forbidden act. To give a warning that this determined course of action constitutes a capital crime is to give to all citizens—including those who consider their execution to be a matter of infinite and distant improbability—a warning that the action in question is regarded by the society to which they belong as particularly detestable: its consequence is to inspire, in regard to this deed, an exceptional aversion and to destroy the temptation to commit it in everyone who fears the reprobation of his fellows. But for professional criminals, those who are tempted to

[1] *The Economist*, 29 December 1855, p. 1428; 17 November 1855, p. 1261.

commit crime and who are on the point of doing so, the fear of death, which it has been the specific aim of the legislator to arouse, exercises only an insignificant influence. The threat of punishment is only one risk added to many others, one further charm in a life of dangers and adventures. The educative effect of capital punishment is real, but its value lies, not in the extent to which it suppresses the guilty or makes him fear his suppression, but in the extent to which it makes him feel the infamy of his deed or, better still, warns him that his fellows think it infamous.[1]

With death all earthly pain, all punishment ceases. The sinner must be allowed to live, that he may suffer and be a warning.[2]

Moreover, asks Hodgskin, has not the death penalty already been virtually abolished?[3] Are not juries beginning to have religious scruples when they see themselves obliged by the law to demand its application?

It is not for us, therefore, and not for any man, to prefer our imagination of what may possibly occur to the plain dictates of morality. We must all endeavour to do right, and trust the issue to HIM in whose hands are the issues of life. . . . The jury at Devizes, as the public at large, find the cherished belief in immortality—in punishment and reward after death—incompatible with inflicting death as a punishment; and sooner or later, partly on account of this incompatibility, it must be given up.[4]

In default of the death penalty, should one pre-

[1] *Ibid.*, 2 May 1857, pp. 475–6.

[2] *Ibid.*, 17 May 1856, pp. 531–2. Cf. 31 May 1856, pp. 587–8.

[3] *Ibid.*, 29 January 1853, pp 114–15.

[4] *Ibid.*, 18 August 1849, pp. 909–10. Cf. 26 January 1856, p. 84.

serve what English law calls "secondary punishment"? Prison? Deportation? Prison creates the old offender, the professional criminal, and modern penal law has not yet discovered means by which society can be rid of him. Moreover, there is one law in political economy, which, in providing for the maintenance of a certain class of men, assures the constant reproduction and regular supply of that particular class. All the money which deportation and prisons cost the state constitutes a perpetual demand for criminals: and for this demand there is a corresponding supply. Prison is "that which feeds crime".[1]

But, to combat crime, modern philanthropy has conceived purely preventive measures, institutions for the "reform" of young prisoners and a general system of state education of the people. Unfortunately the reformatories do not achieve their aim. Children are to be so brought up that they can later win an honest livelihood; but, in the meantime, they are made to live the life of slaves, an existence radically different from their future life as free men.[2] If the question is that of rearing children in a fatherly manner, it would be better to put this in the hands of the parents. "But these parents reared their children badly", it is argued. Too often, Hodgskin answers, because they were poor; and they are still further impoverished by the nation's requirement that they should provide taxation for the maintenance of the reformatories.[3] As to state

[1] *The Economist*, 10 May 1856, pp. 503–4. Cf. 26 April 1856, 25 September 1856, p. 1178.

[2] *Ibid.*, 29 December 1855, pp. 1427–8.

[3] *Ibid.*, 6 September 1856, pp. 981–2.

education, we know that already Hodgskin had declared his hostility to the governmental process of "moralising" the masses, which, to him, was as costly and harmful as other government actions. If statistics prove to a certain extent, he contends, that there is an inverse relationship between the number of criminals and the development of education, what is involved is private education. But the progress of private education, the fact that parents are of their own free will, disposed to give more money for the education of their children, implies a general increase in wealth and popular foresight: and this is the real reason for the diminution in the number of crimes.[1]

We are informed, from the beginning of history, of a gradual progress in knowledge, naturally and necessarily evolved as population increases, bringing with it civilisation, and we hope, certainly, that it may in the end, or at no distant day, teach mankind how to do without constables, soldiers, and gaolers. That kind of progress we see everywhere, and perhaps at all times. Education, or the sedulously drilling of men into a fast adherence to the knowledge already acquired—the training them up to conform to the views or serve the purposes of the educators, we see in Paraguay. Education is, in such cases, all darkness and destruction—the progress of knowledge is all light, life and happiness. But these two different and opposite things, when they approach each other, and education is directed to diffuse some little part of the knowledge continually gathered, are by many people confounded and regarded as one; and the beneficial effects of the natural progress of knowledge are attributed to systems like that of Paraguay, which attempts to check, or altogether stifle it.[2]

[1] *Ibid.*, 12 April 1856, pp. 393–4.

[2] *Ibid.*, 17 April 1847, pp. 433–40. Cf. 10 April 1847, pp. 410–11.

Has one, therefore, to abolish all laws and then expect the immediate and rapid disappearance of all crimes? Hodgskin is not prepared to go this far in his simplification. If the disappearance of the rule of law is the true prescription against the future development of crime, there still remain the existing criminals who are the products of an imperfect state of civilisation. *What shall we do with our criminals?* At the beginning of 1857 Hodgskin approached the problem with a view to reducing it to its simplest terms.[1] He made a distinction between two classes of criminals, those who are met under all conditions and in every kind of community and those who exist in the most civilised and complex societies—the first, guilty by chance or accident, who commit crimes of passion, the others, professional criminals,

> who live by and in crime, who are originally trained in its ranks or are permanently recruited into them, whose avocation and business it is to transgress and to evade the law, to whom society is an enemy and a prey, who steadily in fact follow a profession of which petty larcency is the initiating grade and burglary or coining the culminating honour.

In regard to these latter, the only ones whom Hodgskin would consider, two problems still remained: what to do with the criminals when they had been arrested, and what to do with them when they had been set free, once their punishment had run its course? On these two points Hodgskin proposed to define *principles* and then to examine their *means* of application.

[1] *The Economist*, 31 January 1857. *How to get rid of our criminals*, pp. 110–11.

On the 28th February, Hodgskin dealt with the question of prisons.[1] He called for prisons with cells, since, without cells, prisons, he believed, were schools of crime. He criticised the method of inflicting repeated short terms of imprisonment on those convicted of minor offences, a method which in the end ceased to have any effect on the imagination of the guilty person and turned him into an habitual criminal. On the 2nd May he dealt with the death penalty.[2] But an article on the 16th May which contains an unreserved eulogy of reformatories and denounces "the feeble and morbid humanitarianism fashionable today" is plainly no longer Hodgskin's work.[3] Wilson had just broken with him. Doubtless he had found his articles too doctrinaire for a review concerned with financial and commercial news and too compromising for one whose articles were unsigned; or, more probably and more simply, the doctrines themselves had displeased him. Hodgskin found himself reduced to making a direct appeal to the public and issued invitations to two lectures which he organised on the 20th May and 3rd June at St. Martin's Hall to set forth his wholly negative philosophy of penal law.

At the beginning of his first lecture[4] Hodgskin introduced into his social philosophy a new element which he seems to have borrowed from Carlyle. This factor was imitation.

[1] *Liberated criminals—How crime is fostered*, p. 222.

[2] *The bearing of penal laws on the criminal classes*, pp. 475–6.

[3] *Repression of crime*, pp. 532–3.

[4] *What shall we do with our criminals? Don't create them.* A lecture delivered at St. Martin's Hall, 20 May 1857.

> Man is born in society as he is born a human being. Laws do not create it. He is gregarious like a sheep; and, like the bee, works in common to procure his own and the general sustenance.[1]

Imitation, he said, is a factor universally observable.

> In this condition of mutual dependence, society would only be a succession of conflicts, rubbing itself to pieces, were not men endowed with the means of moulding one another by a reciprocal and silent action; so that all serve the common end of promoting the general welfare.[2]

It is a factor of ever-growing intensity.

> In the progress of society, education, leisure, different pursuits, necessarily confining the attention of each to different objects all tend to make knowledge various and habits conflicting; and this silent influence [of example] is the oil which lessens and destroys the friction of dissimilar individuals and dissimilar classes. The practices of one are imitated by another. Enjoyments are continually equalised. . . . There is a constant tendency to revert to the original equality of mankind, and always to preserve it, while all are improved.[3]

The imitative influence of the upper classes on the lower was the theme with which Hodgskin proposed to deal. From this standpoint he demonstrates that neither nature nor the ruling classes are responsible for the existence of crime but that criminals are "the inevitable result of an erroneous system". *What shall we do with our criminals?* ask the rulers. Hodgskin replies, "*Don't create them*".

The upper classes, he contends, have had the salutary influence over the lower classes of kindling in them a taste for luxury, of increasing their needs

[1] *What shall we do with our criminals ?*, pp. 13–14.
[2] *Ibid.*, p. 14.
[3] *Ibid.*, p. 17.

and, as a result, in the end, of improving their condition. They have in addition, by their example, discredited habits of violence and the practice of murder. But, on the other hand, they have been at all times the ruling class: and it was against the practices of government, the cause and prototype of crime, that Hodgskin, in his second lecture,[1] once more took up his old criticisms.

Positive law, he maintained, is the negation of natural law and, in particular, of the right of property. Law is itself the first of crimes. Consider the method of paying civil servants. In good and bad seasons, in times of prosperity and of crisis, they are sheltered from natural accidents. Nature gives to everyone the produce of his labour, or rather, in the world of exchange, a value equivalent to the value of his produce. But the government wishes to have assured and fixed revenues whatever the product of industry.[2] It decides in consequence to deduct what it pleases from the annual social product. For governments

> the *social* right of property, the *inevitable result of life in society*, inferior in importance and sanctity only to the right of life, and indispensable to the sustenance of all, came to be classed with a court ceremonial, and to be regarded by chancellors of the exchequer as something they could deal with at their pleasure, like a doorkeeper's place at the Treasury.[3]

From this, as a reaction, spring the communist utopias, the denial of the rights of property, the

[1] *Our chief crime: cause and cure.* Second lecture, on what shall we do with our criminals? delivered at St. Martin's Hall, 3 June 1857.

[2] *Ibid.*, p. 20.

[3] *Ibid.*, p. 9.

identification of property with theft. But these two contradictory errors are both destined to disappear.

. . . The people want more food, more clothing, more comforts, more luxuries, more enjoyment, more holidays, more books, more leisure, more intellectual, and fewer animal pursuits. . . . All these wants can only be satisfied by more freedom, and less taxation. The principles announced in 1842, and partially acted on since with such eminent advantage, must be carried into every part of society. The unrestricted competition, which nature establishes, must be the rule for all our transactions; and by the higgling of the market, which is mutual and free action, the salaries of officials, and the payments of the priesthood must be regulated as well as the profit of the shopkeeper, and the wages of the labourer. Society cannot continue united under the sway of two conflicting principles.[1]

Few people attended these meetings and several of those who did were clearly shocked. Hodgskin, in printing his lectures, apologised for their necessarily imperfect and summary character and announced his intention of completing them

by showing, that all legislation, which of course includes Government, is founded on false assumptions. He is preparing for the press a work to be called *The Absurdity Of Legislation Demonstrated*. For a long time the subject has occupied his thoughts and his pen and he proposes to explain his views in a connected didactic form.[2]

But Hodgskin did not publish the projected work, a failure due either to lack of leisure, money, health or time (he was nearly seventy). In January 1859 he

[1] *Our chief crime: cause and cure.* Second lecture on what shall we do with our criminals? delivered at St. Martin's Hall, 3 June 1857. p. 26.

[2] *Ibid.*, p. 26 note.

was still living in the London suburb of Islington and protesting against the legend which attributed the foundation of the Mechanics' Institute to Brougham. In 1860 his youngest daughter was married, the only one of his seven children who had not till then left home.[1] Thereupon he and his wife abandoned their large house, situated in a district which had become densely populated. They set themselves up, first at Hounslow, and then at Feltham. Without completely giving up journalism, Hodgskin had freed himself from the necessity of writing a daily newspaper article; with his son's financial assistance he spent a few peaceful years of old age in the quiet of the countryside. He died on 21 August, 1869, after a few days' illness, at the age of eighty-two. It seems that his compatriots and colleagues had forgotten his existence: not one London newspaper published a notice on his life and works.

[1] [There is a biographical error here. Hodgskin's eldest daughter remained at home with him until his death. (Mary Hodgskin to Halévy, 20 April 1903.) *Translator*]

Conclusion

And so, in oblivion, the history of this unsuccessful career comes to an end. Why did not Hodgskin make the use that he should have done of his capacities as thinker and writer? The reason may be found in that timidity, that lack of confidence in his own powers, from which he had suffered so much as a young man. It may also be suspected that the demands of journalism precluded the concentration of thought necessary for the composition of a work on political economy, on penal law or on the philosophy of history. Account, too, must be taken of historical circumstances. In the years which followed 1832 there was no demand, on the part of an insufficiently enlighted proletariat, for a book setting forth a theory of social economy. The best educated among the workers, a kind of aristocracy of labour, accommodated themselves to the teaching of Ricardo's orthodox followers. Moreover, if it came to tracing a programme of practical action and reform, would the libertarian socialism of Hodgskin be found to differ much from the free-trade philosophy of the Ricardians? Twenty or twenty-five years later, Hodgskin could, if necessary, have developed the anarchist philosophy of history and of society which Spencer and Buckle were to popularise in England. But he was old, Spencer and

Buckle were young: in the same year in which there appeared the strikingly successful first volume of the *History of Civilisation*, Hodgskin, driven from *The Economist*,[1] disappeared into retirement.

Nevertheless his role in the history of ideas is important; and there is perhaps no better example of what value the history of the relationship of ideas provides for the understanding of ideas themselves.

The starting point for Hodgskin's speculations was utilitarian radicalism: but, looked at from a logical point of view, Bentham's system is equivocal, half authoritarian and half libertarian. At one time Bentham takes his stand on the principle of the spontaneous identity of interests to affirm that government should tend to its own annihilation, and to ask that society be left to the natural operation of this beneficent principle. At another he affirms that the function of government is to create artificially the harmony of individual interests by the hope of rewards or, even more, by the fear of punishments. Godwin, in establishing himself solely on the first principle, had already developed the idea of a "society without government". But, when Godwin was writing, Bentham had not yet brought together the two principles in the apparent unity of a system; and the industrialists, the masters of England, had not yet made a success of a doctrine which promised

[1] [Miss Hodgskin subsequently supplied the following note on Hodgskin's departure from *The Economist*. "When Wilson desired the whole spirit of his articles changed, my Father, as on previous similar occasions, simply refused to write anything contrary to his convictions and left the office." (Mary Hodgskin to Halévy, 20 April 1903.)—*Translator*.]

them the abolition of all legal fetters on the spirit of commercial speculation and the drafting of a clear and workable code for the suppression of crimes against property. Hodgskin resurrected Godwin's ideas against those of Bentham. He was the first—before Herbert Spencer—to found a free-trade philosophy on the criticism of the Benthamite philosophy of law. Whereas, Carlyle, in a movement of impassioned reaction against the prevailing current of ideas, placed Benthamism and Cobdenism under the same condemnation, Hodgskin perceived and made clear the contradiction between the two philosophies. He could not concede that it was possible for the radical group to accommodate itself to a policy which was, on the one hand, anti-governmental and liberal and, on the other, administrative and codifying: "society would not long remain submitted to two hostile principles".

But if the ideas of Hodgskin have their starting point in the philosophy of Bentham, it is in the philosophy of Karl Marx, as one knows, that they find their resting place; and it is under their Marxist form that they have gained universal popularisation. Marx had perhaps not yet read Hodgskin when he published his *Poverty of Philosophy*: but, without taking account of the fact that in this work he mentions Thompson, Hodgskin's disciple, it may be noted that he says that he could name many other English economists to support his thesis. In *Capital* he repeatedly cites the three works of Hodgskin in the most important passages of his theory of value. Who knows even whether, between 1850 and 1860, Hodgskin and Marx did not meet personally, both being journalists and living in London, and Hodgskin, furthermore, being connected through his wife with the German colony?

It is impossible, says Marx, to acknowledge that labour is the source and measure of value and, at the same time, to admit, with Ricardo, that wages are the price of labour or measure its value; for if labour measures the value of all commodities it is itself no longer a commodity. Wages, he contends, represent the value, not of labour but of the worker, the source of labour, of labour-power, who, so long as care is taken to make good wear and fatigue, always provides a surplus value. What similarities there are to Hodgskin's theory! According to Hodgskin, Ricardo criticised Adam Smith for having, by turns, defined value as the quantity of labour required to produce commodities and as the quantity of labour which the commodities, once produced, are able to command in the market. Now it is clear, continues Hodgskin, that one cannot, without logical contradiction, consider that the quantity of labour measures the value of commodities when they are exchanged with one another, and that labour itself is exchanged with a commodity; for "labour is not a commodity". But, in Adam Smith's second definition, "substitute the word labourer for the word labour" and then, contends Hodgskin, it perhaps expresses better than the first definition, repeated by Ricardo, the reality of the phenomena of exchange in a society where several economic classes exist and where the capitalist is a person distinct from the worker whom he commands.

But, on the other hand, there are equally striking similarities between the social philosophy of Hodgskin and that of Herbert Spencer, who was his friend and who, perhaps, in certain respects, was influenced by his books and his conversation. Two fundamental ideas, two postulates, or, to use, if one will, an expression of Hodgskin, two "prejudices", are common to Hodgskin and Spencer. Let us try to see to what extent Marx repudiated and to what extent he was influenced by these two prejudices, which we propose to call the anarchist prejudice and the juridical prejudice. This will perhaps be the best means of determining by what bonds—psychological and logical—Marx was connected to the English tradition, excellently represented, before Spencer, by Thomas Hodgskin.

The first "prejudice" of Hodgskin is the anarchist prejudice—that there is a natural law and that, if this is so, the idea of positive law is absurd. All his life this was the fundamental—one is tempted to say the only—theme of Hodgskin's speculations. It is essential to relegate Hodgskin's anti-capitalism to the subordinate place which it always occupied in his system in comparison with his anarchism. His criticism of capitalism was only an incident, an "episode", in the unceasing campaign which he waged against all the privileges of government and against all the oppressions of law. It was to the extent to which he believed that there exist natural and just laws of distribution that Hodgskin contested the false natural laws accepted by the school of Ricardo which were for him the cause of injustice and poverty.

What then is capitalism, the true cause of injustice and poverty? An historical accident, the result of conquest, which cannot upset in any deep or lasting manner the natural balance of economic phenomena. Positive laws can only have an evil action: they can only have an insignificant effect on the permanent laws of nature. These are the two theses of Hodgskin's anarchism.

Certainly, Marx did not, for his part, accept the distinction, familiar to the English school and fundamental to Hodgskin, between the artificial and the natural. He was at one with Hodgskin in criticising the supposed natural laws according to which wealth is divided among the landowner, the capitalist and the wage-earner: but his criticism was not allowed to stop short of the natural law of exchange, respected by Hodgskin and used by him as a basis for his criticism of the laws of the artificial distribution of wealth. For Marx, nature has not for all eternity created autonomous individuals, and taught them how they should exchange the products of their individual labours, the extensions of their personalities, in such a way that each receives the equivalent of the whole produce of his labour. For him, there is nothing permanent in nature, and the only law which it obeys is a law of change. Human society existed before exchange: only in a limited period have individuals, in and through exchange, become separate beings independent of each other. If, subsequently, the primitive game of exchange has been progressively altered by the appropriation of the soil and capitalist accumulation, that is an historical phenomenon, natural and necessary like any other. The capitalist system is itself condemned to perish; but this will not be in order to permit the reappearance of the natural laws, whose operation has been hidden for the moment by the incoherencies of the existing system. When the capitalist system has disappeared, the distribution of wealth will take place according to rules, now unforeseeable, but certainly differing as much from the forms of distribution between autonomous producers as they might differ in other respects from existing forms of distribution.

But whatever difference there may be between the Marxist philosophy of history and the naturalistic optimism of Hodgskin, close similarities are found between them, whether one considers the Marxist theory of value, the Marxist theory of progress or the way in which Marx depicts the final goal to which this progress is leading.

Marx, in his theory of value, regards the differential element as negligible. He considers differential rent as a simple appropriation by the landowner from the profit of the capitalist. Similarly with commercial profit; he, who ended by attaching so great an importance to commercial crises in his philosophy of history, began by demonstrating their theoretical impossibility, only to reintroduce later, and by a roundabout method, the theories of Owen and Sismondi about over-production and the exploitation of the market. Why was there in Marx this tendency at so many points to mitigate the imperfections of the existing distribution of wealth? To understand this it is necessary to go back to Hodgskin or, in a more general way, to the English equalitarian economists. Hodgskin applied himself to lessening the importance of differential rent, expressly justified commercial profit and denied the normality of commercial crises, because to do otherwise would have been to blaspheme against nature. Who, he asked in 1854, is today concerned with what Ricardo wrote about rent? But it was on the basis of the theory of differential rent, enlarged and universalised, that a new socialism was to arise some years later, different from Hodgskin's doctrine and different also, for the same reasons, from Marxist collectivism—a fiscal and interventionist socialism. Hodgskin's anarchist prejudice would preclude his acceptance of this new socialism as legitimate even before he had examined it: and if one thinks of the similarities which exist between the theory of value in Hodgskin and in Marx it can be seen how, as a parallel consequence, Marx's thinking was influenced by the anarchist prejudice.

Moreover, this law of exchange which Marx borrowed from Ricardo and his disciples, both heterodox and orthodox, ceased to have eternal validity for him. Marx's social philosophy is a philosophy of history but, if one tries to find what, in his hypothesis, is the motive force in history, there seems to reappear in Marx the opposition, English in origin, between the reality of nature and the artifices of the mind. According to Marx, only economic development is autonomous. It controls both moral development and legal development, which the idealist philosophers had considered as independent and as each sufficient for its own explanation, but which, in fact, are only the reflections of economic development. Now the English school had taught Marx to isolate economic development from all other developments in this way, to define a world of wealth in which simple mental impulses (*mobiles*) are given a quantitative evaluation and materialise, so to speak, in the form of specie and merchandise, a world half physical but obeying a kind of "natural law": and, before Marx, Hodgskin had established on this conception of an economic world an economic or materialist conception of history. It was vain for Marx to express his historical materialism in Hegelian terms; it was Hume, the master of all the English economists, and in particular of Hodgskin, who had defined the idea as "the copy of an impression". The origin of the Marxist philosophy of history lies in that economic anarchism which is one of Hodgskin's fundamental prejudices.

Economic development will have an end; and this end, Marx, in the same language and for the same reasons as Hodgskin, refuses to define. For the mind cannot anticipate the march of things of which it is the reflection and the copy. It is even difficult to guess, therefore, whether, in the collectivist system, the state will end by absorbing all the functions of society or whether we shall witness the complete annihilation of the state. The nearest one can come to preciseness, perhaps, is to say, in Hegelian terms, that we shall see the absolute identification of these two ends and, in consequence, the simultaneous suppression of both. But Marx, when he speaks of the fall, whether approaching or distant, of capitalism, undoubtedly prefers to speak the language of the anarchist. For in that case no one will any longer demand of the individual—as did Hegel—that he should sacrifice himself or subordinate his identity to the state: the individual will cease to be mystified by the substantial forms of bourgeois political economy, and to believe that land or capital receives a part of the produce of his labour by the inevitable operation of the laws of nature.

But all this is to be found in Hodgskin. Whatever influence the neo-Hegelian anarchism of Bruno Bauer may have exercised on the mind of Marx and the radicalism of Feuerbach on that of Engels, can it be denied that this influence was confirmed and strengthened by the influence of the anarchist economists of London, Hodgskin and his disciple Thompson?

The second of the "inspiring prejudices" of Hodgskin's social philosophy is the one we have called the juridical prejudice. The laws of nature, according to Hodgskin, are beneficent and just, because they give to everyone the whole produce of his labour. But is it not clear how hard and sad a philosophy is concealed under Hodgskin's seeming optimism? It is a philosophy which demands the acceptance of the fact that justice condemns to death the sick, the infirm and the old when their natural vitality fails them; and here the philosophy of Hodgskin comes strangely near to that of Malthus. "Necessity", he tells us, "is the mother of invention, and the continued existence of necessity can only be explained by the continued growth of the people". Would Malthus have expressed himself otherwise?

On this point, however, Hodgskin insists that the consequence of "necessity" is invention and progress. But, we may ask in our turn, is not that a roundabout way of saying, with Malthus, that invention and progress depend on "necessity", on poverty, and on "unending" poverty? Moreover, is the right of everyone to the product of his labour anything other than the right of force? And is not this implicitly acknowledged by Hodgskin? Wishing to show that nature herself teaches the respect of the labour of others in her products, he takes his stand on the principle that nature gives to the man, who has the strength to produce, sufficient strength also to defend the produce of his labour. The right to the whole produce of labour is the right of force appeased and controlled. The jurist admits the struggle between conflicting egoisms to be legitimate on condition that individuals observe the rule of expending their strength, not in struggling directly against each other, but in struggling directly against nature, and only indirectly against one another to the extent to which some find themselves able to take advantage of others. After which, to arrive at the conclusion that nature is just, it is sufficient to leave out of account all the natural monopolies and to suppose that nature confers success on whosoever, by more intense labour or greater ingenuity, has most lowered the cost of production. Thus for open and lawless warfare there is substituted a well ordered struggle, a rivalry, better still, a competition; but in the last analysis, war always remains the law of life. Either Hodgskin has to reinstate the family sentiments in his psychology as natural sentiments (and this in fact is what he does, though at the cost of violating the principle of his philosophy of law; and in so doing he comes closer to the orthodox economists) or else his system, which consists in the elimination of all the communist elements in existing society, ends not in socialism but in a more extreme individualism.

But the principle according to which everyone would have the right to the whole produce of his labour is certainly not the principle of Marxist philosophy. According to Marx, this juridical ideal might be realised by some governmental institution through which every individual would receive a quantity of the product of national labour corresponding to the duration of the labour which he himself provided. But to do this would be to forget that the Ricardian theory of labour-value is only realised in and through free exchange; it would favour the idler at the expense of the industrious worker, and its outcome would be the decline of production and the impoverishment of the human race. So far Marx is in agreement with Hodgskin. Alternatively, one could count on the capitalist anomaly eliminating itself to permit the natural working of exchange and the restoration to everyone of the value produced by his work. But to argue thus involves a lack of historical sense: it is to forget that the mechanism of exchange has naturally produced capitalist accumulation and that, if capitalism disappears in its turn, it will give place to a new system as different from the system of exchange as from capitalism itself. And it is on this point that Marx parts company with Hodgskin.

The economic interpretation of history, moreover, allows of the explanation of the origin of this supposed juridical idea. It is, like every human ideal, the reflection of an economic reality. Men, in exchanging commodities in proportion to the quantities of labour which they contain, have translated this fact of material life into a legal theory. Let the system of exchange once disappear, and this juridical ideal will become devoid of meaning as it will become devoid of its object.

Finally, it is only within restricted limits, according to Marx, that objects are exchangeable with one another in proportion to the amount of labour involved in their production. In the first place, man has in some manner to do violence to nature to reduce different qualities of labour to a common conventional denominator. Only with time and the development of machinery does labour tend to become a naturally homogeneous quantity. But by this time the capitalist system has developed, and when capitalists exact equal profits for equal quantities of capital engaged in different enterprises, the labour theory of value once again is not strictly applicable.

However, in spite of this last limitation, the labour theory of value is clearly the Marxist theory of value. This theory was borrowed directly by Marx from Ricardo. Undoubtedly he proposed to refute Ricardo; and we are aware what essentially dialectic or historical method he applied to the refutation of economic systems. There is no theory which is true for all time, but neither is there any theory which is eternally false. Time successively sanctifies and condemns systems. A false theory is one that has ceased to be true and which, being the reflection of a certain group of economic phenomena, has become without meaning from the day when the social reality to which it corresponds has ceased to exist, ruined by internal contradictions. So that, in order to refute Ricardo's political economy, Marx believes that first he has to establish that it is true for the world of exchange, that it is "the scientific expression of economic relations in existing society". If, moreover, it is never true except in an approximate and imperfect fashion, that is because the mechanism of exchange, constantly changed by the intervention of disturbing elements, tends to come into being only to be immediately destroyed. But the question arises whether one is right in according even this partial justification to the Ricardian theory. It is true, but it will cease to be true: that is what Marx tells us. But what if it happened to be false? Ricardo himself came to doubt whether his theory was the precise expression of the phenomena of exchange. About 1825 it would perhaps have been amended in England by Malthus, Samuel Bailey and others, had not an intransigent group of Ricardo's disciples succeeded in stifling all the disagreements surrounding Ricardo through their active propaganda and the very simplicity of their teaching. Another cause, however, contributed to the triumph of the theory. The democratic opponents of James Mill and MacCulloch, the first working-class theorists, instead of attacking the Ricardian theory of value, seized upon its principle to draw from it new conclusions and to refute, by a form of *reductio ad absurdum*, Ricardo's political economy. This became a kind of universal obsession of which Karl Marx, twenty years later, could not but be the victim.

But, on one point, the teaching of the Ricardian socialists is of great value to the historian of ideas; for it, and it alone, informs us of the true psychological origin of the labour theory of value. That commodities are exchanged in proportion to the quantity of labour which they have cost to produce is given by Adam Smith and Ricardo as an evident fact, a kind of axiom or postulate of a new geometry; and it is quite impossible to accept the dialectical argument, by which Marx seems to wish to establish this proposition, as a proof of it. But Hodgskin, a philosopher at the same time as he is an economist, finds the true source of the labour theory of value in Locke. If men exchange their products in proportion to the quantities of labour which they have cost, it is to the extent to which they feel dimly that every one naturally has a right to the whole produce of his labour. In other words, from the teaching of Hodgskin it emerges that the classical theory of value in exchange is the reflection, not of present economic reality, but of a preconceived juridical ideal. If Marx, in a certain measure at least, has made it his own, has he not been the unknowing and indirect victim of this same juridical prejudice, in spite of his efforts to destroy it? Hodgskin's theory, considered in this way, is insufficient to refute Marx's philosophy; but it is sufficient, certainly, to cast a legitimate suspicion upon the dialectic apparatus with which Marx surrounds it.

Bibliography

I. Works of Thomas Hodgskin

1. *An Essay on Naval Discipline, showing part of its evil effects on the minds of the officers and the minds of the men and on the community; with an amended system by which Pressing may be immediately abolished*, London, 1813.
2. *Travels in the North of Germany, describing the present state of the Social and Political Institutions, the Agriculture, Manufactures, Commerce, Education, Arts and Manners in that Country, particularly in the Kingdom of Hanover*, Edinburgh, 1820.
3. *Labour defended against the claims of capital; or, the unproductiveness of capital proved with reference to the present combinations amongst journeymen*, by a labourer; London, 1825.
4. *Popular political economy*, four lectures delivered at the London Mechanics' Institution, London, 1827.
5. *The natural and artificial right of property contrasted, a series of letters, addressed without permission, to H. Brougham, esq. M.P., F.R.S., etc. (now the Lord Chancellor)*, by the author of *Labour defended against the claims of capital*, London, 1832.
6. *What shall we do with our criminals? Don't create them.* A lecture, delivered at St. Martin's Hall, 20 May 1857, by Thomas Hodgskin.
7. *Our chief crime: cause and cure.* Second lecture, on what shall we do with our criminals? delivered at St. Martin's Hall, 3 June 1857.
8. A certain number of articles appeared in the course of the first year (1823) of the *Mechanics' Magazine*. Programme (30 August); On the Spitalfields Acts (6 September and 4 October); Formation of the Mechanics' Institute (11 and 25 October).

9. A series of articles appeared between 1844 and 1857 in *The Economist*. A list of these follows, from which, however, there may be omissions:

1844 Connection between poverty and crime (12 October).

1846 The Punishment of Death (16 and 23 May).
Reviews of
D. Ricardo, *Principles of Political Economy* (ed. MacCulloch) (28 November).
Anon., *Outlines of Social Economy* (12 December).
G. R. Porter, *Progress of the Nation* (19 December).

1847 National systems of Education (20 March).
Shall the State educate the people? (3 April).
Education and Crime (10 and 17 April).
The Education question—Mr. Macaulay (24 April).
Adam Smith rescued from Mr. Macaulay (1 May).
What is to be done with our criminals? (24 July).

1848 Increase of pauperism and crime (17 June).
Presumption of the literary classes (21 October).
Mr. Macaulay's Philosophy (30 December).
Reviews of
G. Poulett Scrope, *The Rights of Industry* (29 April).
Stuart Mill, *The Principles of Political Economy* (27 May).
H. C. Carey, *The Past, the Present and the Future* (28 October).
W. A. McKinnon, *The History of Civilisation and Public Opinion* (30 December).

1849 Marriages and Abundance (26 May).
Punishment of death (18 August).
Reviews of
Andrew Coventry Dick, *The Nature and the Office of the State* (20 January).
Edward Kellogg, *Labour and other Capital* (17 March).

Introduction to the study of the social sciences, by the author of the *Outlines of Social Economy* (26 May).

Hepworth Dixon, *John Howard and the Prison World of Europe* (15 September).

Joseph Fletcher, *Summary of the moral statistics of England and Wales* (22 September).

1850 Scarcity—Marriages, Births (2 February).

Education of the People (2 March).

Law and Justice (30 March).

National Education (18 May).

Criminal Returns (22 June).

Scarcity and Criminality—France and Germany (29 June).

Diminished Criminality (20 July).

The Diffusion of Wealth (10 August).

1851 Educational schemes (24 May).

Pauperism and free trade (24 May).

Education, pauperism and crime (31 May).

Criminals in England and Wales, 1850 (9 August).

Pauperism—July returns—prosperity of the country (16 August).

Pauperism and distress formerly and now (23 August).

Increase of population and decrease of criminality (13 September).

Reviews of

Herbert Spencer, *Social Statistics* (8 February).

James Hole, *Lectures on social science and the organisation of labour* (1 March).

Th. Plint, *Crime in England* (23 August).

George Opdyke, *A treatise on political economy* (22 November).

J. R. MacCulloch, *A treatise on the rate of wages* (27 December).

1852 National Education (17 January).

Education question (7 February).

The Protectionist Policy, Mr. Henley (13 March).

Decrease of pauperism and criminality (27 March).
The Punishment of Death (27 March).
Diminution of Crime and Pauperism (17 July).
Marriages, Births and Deaths (31 July).
Ireland — Improvement — Criminals — Paupers (21 August).
Mr. Henley and Pauperism (2 October).
Marriages, Births and Deaths (6 November).
Reviews of
John Lalor, *Money and Morals* (17 July).
George Cornewall Lewis, *Methods of observation and reasoning in politics* (27 November).

1853 The Task of Government: the disposal of our criminal population (29 January).
Continual decrease of pauperism (5 March).
The Ministerial Plan of Education (3 April).
Crime in 1852 (14 May).
Pauperism—Ireland and England (2 July).
Reduction of Pauperism (24 September).
Review of
R. Hildreth, *Theory of Politics* (20 August).

1854 Increase of Pauperism (18 February).
Further Increase of Pauperism (26 August).
Too much care taken of criminals (30 September).
Criminals—England and Wales. Increased criminality of females (28 October).
The criminal returns (4 November).
Reviews of
Morrison, *An Essay on the relations between Labour and Capital* (29 April).
The Works of Locke (St-John edition) (16 September).
George K. Rickards, *Population and Capital* (18 November).
Charles Knight, *Knowledge is power* (30 December).

1855 Increase of Pauperism (3 March).
Pauperism—Emigration (19 May).

The Morality of trade and of law (23 June).
Pauperism—Ireland (23 June).
Messrs. Strahan and Co. and their Defence (30 June).
Marriages, births and deaths, quarterly returns (4 August).
Pauperism (18 August).
What shall we endow? (25 August).
Committal of Messrs. Strahan, Paul and Bates (15 September).
Pauper removals and popular emigration (29 September).
The conviction of Paul, Strahan and Bates (3 November).
Quarterly returns of marriages (10 November).
Methods of moral improvement (10 November).
What stands in the way of improvement? (17 November).
New reformatories for criminals (29 December).
Reviews of
E. R. Humphreys, *A Manual of Political Science;* Richard Jennings, *Natural Elements of Political Economy* (23 June).

1856 Population, wealth, criminality (12 January).
Murder and punishment of death (26 January).
Invasions of property (1 and 8 March).
Criminals—England and Wales (8 March).
Pauperism—Ireland (8 March).
Continued increase of pauperism (15 March).
Relations between crime and material welfare (15 March).
Relations between crime and the distribution of wealth (22 March).
The sources of Crime—Drunkenness (29 March).
Report of Prison Inspectors (12 April).
Transportation (26 April).
What feeds crime? (10 May).

Shall executions be public, private or abolished? (17 May).
Palmer—a great culprit (31 May).
Expense of Pauperism (31 May).
The Philosophy of Legislation (7 June).
Marriages and commitments (14 June).
Criminality promoted by distress (21 June).
Criminals—Ireland—1855 (19 July).
Criminality and poverty in Ireland (26 July).
Criminal statistics (23 August).
Decrease of Pauperism (23 August).
The proposed Reformatories (6 September).
Transportation—Report of the Committee (13 September).
Ireland—Census, Cultivation, etc. (13 September).
What feeds crime? (25 October).
An admitted effect of Reformatories (6 December).
Criterion of law reform. Means of determining social rights (13 December).
Criminal law reform (20 December).

1857 How to get rid of our criminals (31 January).
Liberated criminals. How crime is fostered (28 February).
The bearing of penal laws on the criminal classes (2 May).

10. Hodgskin's letters to Francis Place 1817–23 (Unpublished). See F. Place, Private Correspondence, Vol. II, 1817–37. Brit. Mus. Add. MSS. 35, 153, ff. 52–215.

II. Manuscript Sources and Secondary Authorities.

1. The Place Papers in the British Museum.
   (a) Private Correspondence, Vol. I, 1810–16 (Add. MSS. 35, 152, ff. 141, 184, 195, 229), and Vol. II (see above).
   (b) School Institutions, Add. MSS. 27, 823—Early History of the London Mechanics' Institution, 1823–26 (f. 240 ff.).

(c) Political Narratives, Vol. III, Add. MSS. 27, 791—Historical Sketch of the National Union of the Working Classes, to 31 December 1831 (especially ff. 268–70: biographical information about Hodgskin).

2. The following works by contemporaries of Hodgskin:
   Samuel Read, *Natural Grounds of Right to Vendible Property*, 1829.
   Thomas Cooper, *Lectures on the Elements of Political Economy*, 2nd ed., 1830.
   Charles Knight, *The Rights of Industry*, 1831 (Three refutations of Hodgskin).
   John Lalor, *Money and Morals, a book for the times*, 1852 (Commendatory reference to Hodgskin in the Preface, p. xxiv; extracts from *Labour Defended* in an appendix).

3. In A. Menger, *Das Recht auf den vollen Arbeitsertrag in geschichtlicher Darstellung*, a simple mention of the name in a note (2nd ed., pp. 52–3 note). Misled by an error of Engels (*Capital*, Book II, Preface) Menger blamed Marx for having written "Hopkins" for "Hodgskin" in his *The Poverty of Philosophy*. But Hopkins, the author of the *Economical enquiries relative to the laws which regulate rent, profit, wages, and the value of money*, 1822, was a socialist, or at least a pre-socialist, writer. In the English translation by Tanner, see the introduction and bibliography by H. S. Foxwell, p. lv ff. See also Graham Wallas, *Life of Francis Place*, 1898, and G. Goddard, *George Birkbeck, the pioneer of popular education*, 1884.

Bibliographical Addendum

(*by* A. J. Taylor)

The following additional published works of Thomas Hodgskin may be noted:

1. *The Word BELIEF defined and explained*, London, 1827.
2. *Peace, Law and Order.* A lecture delivered in the Hall of the National Association, on 29 September, 1842. London, undated.
3. *A lecture on free trade in connexion with the corn laws*, delivered at the White Conduit House, on 31 January, 1843. London, 1843.
4. *A letter to Richard Cobden, M.P. on free-trade and slave labour.* London, 1848.

THE WORD *BELIEF* DEFINED AND EXPLAINED

This essay, Hodgskin's only purely philosophical work, merits a brief comment. It was written, as he indicates in the preface, from a "particular motive", a motive which he makes explicit in a letter to Joseph Hume, M.P., soliciting the latter's support for his (Hodgskin's) candidature for a "Professor's Chair in the London University".[1] (The chair—in moral philosophy—was never filled.) The essay can, therefore, be regarded as being, in the strict sense of the term, a masterpiece. Its argument may be conveniently summarised in the following passages:

(1) "bodily sensations, perceptions, remembered and imagined notions, with suggestions of the understand-

[1] Hodgskin to J. Hume, undated letter (1827), bound in Hume Tracts i. 39 (University College London Library).

ing and deductions of reason, our chief feelings, all produce actions, and are all equally believed in the philosophical sense of the term. We are not conscious of them, and of another distinct and separate feeling accompanying some of them only, called belief, as is generally stated by metaphysicians; we are conscious only of the sensations. Thus belief, in metaphysics, is only another term for feeling." (p. 22.)

(2) "Belief in assertions then, only means, that we are conscious of the feelings which words excite, and that they are not contradicted by feelings more continually excited. Disbelief on the contrary, means that we are conscious of some other feelings, with which those excited by words do not correspond . . . (p. 27). It is from a multitude of events preceding any simple event, and all of them preceding it in the same order, that we are led to make the separation, to doubt which is the constant antecedent, and to endeavour to find it by diligent observation." (p. 45.)

(3) ". . . The phenomena of consciousness will have to be treated in the same manner as the phenomena of the physical world. . . . The inquiry into the laws of our belief, which since the days of Berkeley, has so much engaged the attention of philosophers, can on these principles mean nothing more than an inquiry into the existence of our feelings, and into the order in which they arise; including those which are universally and continually excited in all men; and those which arise only at some moments in some individuals." (p. 47.)

This essay is noteworthy for clarity of exposition rather than for originality of thought. Hodgskin clearly identifies himself with the Scottish school of Thomas Reid, Dugald Stewart and Thomas Brown,[1] a school to which the Mills were also much indebted. Hodgskin would appear to have been most strongly influenced by

[1] "I purpose to point out the facts of our mental constitution, now represented by the word belief, as Dr. T. Brown has pointed out, the facts signified by the terms cause, power and will" (p. 3).

Brown—he may indeed have attended his lectures in 1819. He cites Brown with approval on a number of occasions and shares with him a critical doubt of Hume's assertion that belief in the inevitable relation between specific causes and specific effects springs from "experience and custom" (p. 44): but he differs from Brown in asserting that belief is synonymous and not merely concomitant with feeling.

In spite of his German travels and of his knowledge of the German language, Hodgskin appears to have had no acquaintance with the great new German philosophical school of Kant and Hegel.

The following books published since Halévy's *Thomas Hodgskin* are concerned in part with Hodgskin.

H. P. G. Quack, *De Socialisten. Personen en stelsels. Een groep vergeten figuren uit het Engeland der vorige eeuw* . . . (Hodgskin's *Labour Defended* vertaald door J. de Hoop Scheffer) (Amsterdam, 1904).

Esther Lowenthal, *The Ricardian Socialists* (New York, 1911).

Carl Keopp, *Das Verhältnis der Mehrwertheorien von Karl Marx und Thomas Hodgskin* (Vienna, 1911).

Max Beer, *The History of British Socialism* (English edition, London, 1920).

G. H. Schütze, *Die Lehre von der Verteilung in der Volkwirtschaft bei Thomas Hodgskin. Ein dogmenkritischer Versuch* (Leipzig, 1930).

C. H. Driver, "Thomas Hodgskin and the Individualists", *Social and Political Ideas of the Age of Reaction and Reconstruction* (ed. Hearnshaw) (London, 1931), pp. 191–219.

H. L. Beales, *The Early English Socialists* (London, 1933).

W. Stark, *The Ideal Foundations of Economic Thought* (London, 1943).

Alexander Gray, *The Socialist Tradition* (London, 1944).

G. D. H. Cole, *Socialist Thought, the Forerunners* (London, 1952).

Index

Printed in Great Britain by
Western Printing Services Ltd. Bristol

DATE DUE
